# HOW TO ENJOY BIBLE STUDY WITH OTHERS

# HOW TO ENJOY BIBLE STUDY WITH OTHERS

*by*
Rice A. Pierce

Thomas Nelson Inc.
Nashville and New York

*To the most lively,
Bible-respecting Sunday School class of men
I know anything about!*

ISBN Number: 0-8407-5043-9

Library of Congress Catalog Card Number: 72-5250

Printed in the United States of America

# *Contents*

# HOW TO ENJOY BIBLE STUDY WITH OTHERS

# CHAPTER 1
## *Enjoyment Is . . .*

"I just don't enjoy Sunday School anymore, Paul. That's why I don't come. Something's happened to the class. It's not like it used to be. Maybe it's me, but I just don't enjoy it."

Do people like you and me really want to enjoy their Bible study with others? Do they feel there is *anything* that will help them enjoy Sunday School more?

A recent extensive survey of church members revealed that 69 percent of these persons would like Sunday School far more if there were better class involvement and participation in the Bible study.* This feeling on the part of class members does not mean any lessening of the teacher's role in Sunday School. It does highlight the truth that good class members make good teachers. The class in which the most stimulating Bible teaching takes place is the class where the members help most to make the experience

*See *Understanding Adults* by Lucien E. Coleman, Jr. (Nashville: Convention Press, 1969), chapter 5.

spiritually satisfying. The good class member respects his teacher, supports him, prays for him, and regards him with Christian love.

Bible study for any group of concerned persons is such a holy undertaking that every member of the group is called upon to be his best. For it is in this kind of inclusive, purposeful study that God's will is revealed to one who would find guidance and joy in Bible study with others.

## Bible Study is Meant to Be Enjoyed

General Robert E. Lee once was asked by an aide what he thought of a certain officer in his command. "Why, that man is one of the bravest officers I have," Lee replied. "That's strange," replied the aide. "He thinks very little of you and doesn't mind saying so." "You asked my opinion of him, Sir," Lee replied, "not his opinion of me."

We are not going to look right now at what some people today think about Bible study with others. We are going to examine the Bible's own opinion of the joy its study is supposed to bring to believers.

Look through your Bible and find the many places where the pleasure of encounter with God's Word is mentioned. Jeremiah said that when God's words came to him, they brought joy to his heart (Jeremiah 15:16). The psalmist encouraged believers to be glad in the Lord, and rejoice (Psalm 32:11). They were to serve (hear?)

the Lord with gladness (Psalm 100:2). The psalmist delighted in what he had learned about God and his precepts (Psalm 119:14–16, 162,167). "I rejoice at thy word." Joy comes from studying God's Word, then going to carry out its teachings (Psalm 126:6). When believers get together, said Paul, peace, joy, and happiness should describe their relationships (Romans 14:17; 15:13, 24; Ephesians 5:18). The Bereans eagerly studied the Scriptures together in order to satisfy themselves about what they had heard (Acts 17:11).

So our Sunday School class is not supposed to be a dose of medicine, an ordeal, a boring time to sit out until the bell rings, a time for dozing and daydreaming. Christ wants us to *enjoy* our Bible study with others!

## Enjoyment Is—Satisfaction

A friend of mine used to tell about Little Billy who had received a very large book from Granny for his birthday. Granny had heard that Billy was expressing an interest in the Antarctic and especially in penguins. So she sent him the huge volume.

Dutifully Billy wrote his thank-you note:
"Dear Granny,
    Thank you very much for the book you
    sent me. It is very interesting. But it
does tell me more about penguins than I really want to know."
We are not going to discuss more about Bible

study than you really want to know, hopefully. But enjoyment is many things when you reflect upon the good feelings that come to you from Bible study with others. Of course, you do not enjoy all the things all the time that we are about to consider. Nor does every class member enjoy in each of these ways to the same degree that you may feel it. But enjoyment *is* all these things, and more, to some people some of the time. And these experiences make Bible study all the richer because of them.

Enjoyment is *satisfaction*. It is satisfaction about the accuracy and completeness of Bible facts that are brought out. You hear the teacher say that David had "a lot of problems" in trying to be a good father to the boy Absalom. And you wonder: *Problems? What problems?* Or a class member says that Absalom showed his depraved character: "He tried to murder" his father David. Again you wonder: *Tried to murder? Or did he stir up a rebellion? Is there a difference?* If you are thinking at all (and you are!), you simply enjoy Sunday School more when facts are clarified to your satisfaction.

But other satisfactions contribute to your enjoyment of Bible study. A class member says, for instance, that you can't put too much stock in the David-Absalom story: men lived in rougher ways then. Or, God did let David and Bathsheba live together after their first baby died, but he deals with people differently today. You sit there in your chair in the class and wonder: *Is this really a correct interpretation of what the Bible teaches? Isn't God's Word closer to the truth for today than this? What is the meaning?*

You enjoy Sunday morning Bible study more, also, when you are satisfied about what you hear concerning convictions and commitment to God. For instance, your teacher may say: "When I study the life of David, frankly I can't explain how a man who sinned like David did could be called by the Bible a man after God's own heart." You aren't satisfied, somehow, with this statement about what full commitment to God means. You won't be really happy with this Bible study until this question is worked out for you.

Finally, enjoyment is being satisfied about the response you make to God's Word and his will. Your fellow class members have done a good job of trying to see God's Word as it is. They have made a genuine acceptance of what the Scripture passage teaches. But you are sitting in your chair and thinking in all honesty: *What do we do in order to obey God as we have heard him speak through his Word this morning?* Enjoyment is being satisfied about what you and your class are going to *do* in ministry and witness as a result of your Bible study.

These are some of the satisfactions which make Bible study with others enjoyable. Fortunate are you when your class experiences offer them.

## Being Silent

At this point you may be a little like the first-grader who proudly showed his mother the gold star he had earned at school. "We get these for what we do best," he explained. "And what do you do best?" she asked. "I'm the best rester!" beamed the boy.

This book, it is true, is mostly about *not* resting, about not being silent in the Sunday School class. But enjoyment for you is, nevertheless, being silent at times during the study. You even may want to spend the whole class time in silence once in a while in order to truly enjoy your study. (Or you may want to be silent *most* of the time—every session. So be it!) But the topic at times simply may be one which you do not feel emotionally or spiritually ready to discuss with others. Or you may remain quiet the first part of the session because you remember how much you talked last time. Or you may regret something you have just said and so now you are going to "do penance" by staying quiet for a while. So you listen.

But you can enjoy just listening, also, simply because the teacher and others are saying things you didn't know. It is good to hear what they are saying. Or maybe your idea of the biblical picture isn't clear yet. It is satisfying to hear others try to discover the Bible meaning. And, too, your silence may mean that you are simply praying and reflecting. After all, if Christ is in your midst when even two or three are gathered together, just his presence brings the deepest joy you can experience. Nothing else need happen for the moment. Whatever the personal reason you may have for being silent when you might be speaking, you are meeting a deep need at this time by your silence. And it brings you enjoyment.

## Being Accepted

"I have never been in a Sunday School class before in my life where I was immediately accepted and made to feel at home like I have been received here," a fifty-year-old man said to his inwardly rejoicing teacher.

You can be vocal or silent in a discussion-type Sunday School class and still be "accepted." Enjoyment is being accepted by the class whether you are silent or whether you "put your foot in your mouth" every time you speak. You enjoy being with a class of men or women—or both— when they welcome and respect you as you are. They don't have to like everything you say or do, but they welcome you as part of the Bible study group. They may disagree with you more often than they agree with you. But it is your statement that they question, not your presence. And when you are absent, they express concern. Enjoyment is being in a class which accepts you in the name of Christ.

## Expressing Yourself

Don't you enjoy being in a group where you feel free to say what you think? or what you feel? Isn't it good to be in a Sunday School class where teacher and members speak the truth? (Truth is not only what the Bible says; it is what the Bible *means*. Truth is how people *are,* not just how they ought to be.) Openness (amid trust and kindness) is true enjoyment. Even a *little* openness in a Bible class is more enjoyable than none. Directness—in love—is refreshing from the Sunday School teacher. And the joy which Paul and the other biblical writers spoke about comes partly from this freedom to express yourself honestly and still feel relaxed, basically at peace with your fellow class members.

Honest interaction in Bible study brings a dimension of reality and enjoyment which can be experienced in no other way. What if you are in a class with young and older adults mixed? And what if all of you *do* speak back and forth frankly about what David owed to Absalom and what Absalom owed to David? Cannot truth, understanding, and peace between generations result from this kind of Bible study? And eventually, more joy?

## *Being Appreciated*

A father of two teen-agers said to his Sunday School teacher: "You know, I try to express to my children what loyalty to Christ means, and I try to help the men who work with me to acknowledge the value of the individual's commitment to Christ. But the only place I feel that these convictions are appreciated is here in our class."

Is there a difference between being accepted in the class and being appreciated? Especially after we have expressed ourselves? Possibly yes. Maybe you can feel genuinely accepted by Sunday School members when first joining the group, without feeling appreciated as much as you may feel later. But a deeper enjoyment in Bible study comes when your teacher and other class members do show that they appreciate you. That is, you have been yourself, expressed yourself, and members begin to let you know that they feel something of your worth.

## *Being Prepared*

Enjoyment of Bible study—or of any other learning experience—increases when you are ready for what is to follow. Do you remember the agony of going to take a test in school when you knew you weren't ready? But how about that carefree, anticipating, almost happy feeling when you *knew you were prepared* and you were just waiting to face your teacher and "give it back to him."

Fortunately for us today, showing that we are prepared does not always mean that we simply are asked to "give it back" just the way it was written. Being prepared today (even for Bible study) means being ready—with some facts, yes— but also with thoughts, reflections, convictions, experiences to share. And deep enjoyment comes when we get together with others and are able to reveal that we have valued the occasion enough to prepare for responsible participation. Is all this too heavy a way of saying that it is agony to feel unready for an approaching experience, but joy to feel that you are ready for what is about to happen in Bible study?

## Setting Goals

You may say that thinking of objectives you want to reach in Bible study with others is too much like eating spinach because it's good for you. But, actually, isn't it fun deciding what you would like to do—in *any* area of living? True, this selecting what you want to do and what you want to be is a more serious side of joy in living. But how unhappy would you be if you never did set goals for yourself in areas of living that are important to you? And so enjoyment is indeed this seeking more understanding, gaining stronger convictions, obeying Christ more faithfully in and through Bible study with others. This kind of purposefulness is a breakthrough in what we do about learning today, for which we truly can rejoice.

## Expressing Enthusiasm

An elderly woman in one of pioneer Methodist preacher Peter Cartwright's classes, it is said, sometimes would upset him with her spiritual enthusiasm. On one occasion the aged saint exclaimed: "Oh, if I had one more feather in the wing of my faith, I would fly away and be with my Savior!"

"Stick in the other feather, Lord," quickly responded Cartwright, "and let her go."

Expressing yourself in Sunday School may not always mean expressing enthusiasm. And yet there is joy in feeling enthusiasm for your Bible study and in expressing it. The more you express enthusiasm in Sunday School, the more you feel enthusiasm and enjoy what you are doing. Can you feel happy over the Bible study experiences you have in your class? Your enjoyment is increased when you express this enthusiasm during discussion or later to your teacher.

## *Thinking*

It is fun to think. If you don't believe this, try not thinking for a while. Enjoyment is hearing what is being said and pondering what you think about it. The mind is one of those possessions God gave us when he fashioned us in his image. We gain inner confidence and pleasure from exercising this mind, especially upon the truth taught in God's Word.

Even children experience this satisfaction of thinking and of expressing the understanding they have gained. A little girl once sat with her mother in the worship service. The preacher was trying to convince his listeners of the reality of God. "Why, he is as near as the next room," said the minister. "Why does he say that?"

whispered the wondering but happy child. "God is right here beside us, isn't he?"

To sit and listen unthinkingly to "talk" about God and the Scriptures may not be a sin, but it surely is boring! The opposite of this experience is to hear biblical facts alertly; to weigh interpretations thoughtfully; to feel pro or con about expressions of conviction; to decide with care about the response to Bible truth that is being discussed.

You know how good it feels to stretch your muscles when you've been sitting still a long time. This same good feeling comes when you stretch your mind in the kind of Bible study that requires you to think. The satisfaction which we considered earlier in this chapter comes more fully when you are being part of a "thinking" man's Bible study. To solve thoughtfully one's spiritual problems brings enjoyment to the soul.*

## *Giving and Taking*

No, we are not about to say that a free-for-all in Sunday School is a good thing. But we do say that enjoyment is being in the class, taking a Bible concept, and speaking—listening —speaking again—listening again. When you are thinking, praying, expressing yourself, listening, appreciating—this give-and-take with others over some difficult spiritual problem in the Bible becomes exciting!

---

*See *Blueprint for Teaching* by John T. Sisemore (Nashville: Broadman Press, 1964), p. 79.

Discovering today's meaning of God's Word can be fun. Especially when the mental and emotional involvement raises the classroom temperature at least up to the enthusiasm level (not the debate level). And it is this give-and-take between teacher and class member and between class members themselves that brings spiritual excitement.

## Helping Achieve Oneness

Only Satan and his spokesmen want disharmony and fractured fellowship in a church or Sunday School class. Christians seek harmony and oneness in their groups. Jesus prayed to the Father that all the different kinds of persons who should become his followers would be one (John 17:20–21).

The teacher of one men's class in the church was also chairman of deacons. The church was facing a difficult problem which could seriously harm its fellowship. Some of the deacons who had taken a strong position were in the class. The teacher prayed about the matter and talked with a trusted member of the class who also was a deacon. Then the teacher "opened up" the issue on Sunday morning when it came naturally out of the Bible study. During discussion, disturbed deacons were listened to and a reconciling approach to the problem emerged as class members talked things out. A crisis with the pastor at the next deacon's meeting was avoided. Harmony in Christ is happiness. And there is deep enjoyment in helping your fellow class members find this oneness. We are not talking about sameness of thought and feeling in everything, of course. Every class member's life situation is different. The Bible speaks the same message in different ways to each person. Each member around you in the class is at a different stage of spiritual development. Thus what your neighbor hears a Scripture passage say is different in some way from what you hear. But deep pleasure comes from helping your class achieve oneness of *spirit* toward one another, helping them gain a general atmosphere of loving support for one another's concerns, purposes, and efforts at commitment to Christ.

## Experiencing Variety

Who likes monotony? Gaines S. Dobbins says that the poorest Bible study approach that a class can use is "the one used all the time!" *

Isn't it fun to be in a Sunday School class where you can't predict every time exactly how the Bible study will go? And what about this wonderful mind (believe it or not) that God has given you? It takes mental and emotional challenges of many kinds in order for your mind and heart to thrill you with what they can do in response to God's Word.

Of course, it's true that one person will learn

---

* *Leading Dynamic Bible Study* by Rice A. Pierce (Nashville: Broadman Press, 1969), p. 6.

better when the Bible study is approached one way, while another can respond better to a different approach. (This is the teacher's problem.) But do you not enjoy your classroom study more at one time in a certain way, and at another time in another way? Your mood varies greatly, and not just from a whim. Sometimes you just don't feel like discussion, or a lecture. And so variety brings enjoyment to Bible study.

## Practicing Adaptability

Closely related to the spiritual pleasure of finding variety in Bible study is that of practicing adaptability. Circumstances in the class change from one meeting to the next. The situation changes even during a session. You feel good at being able to help now one way, now another. For then you are being your best for Christ as you aid your class through its varying experiences of serious, loving Bible study.

Have you ever "risen to the occasion" of a crisis in the class, with the Holy Spirit's help? Weren't you happy at what God's grace had enabled you to do? Or maybe your class was forced to go out and meet under a tree. Isn't it fun to possess and demonstrate the adaptability to go on and enter into thoughtful Bible study, no matter what the physical circumstances are? You enjoy the feeling that your teacher can count on you to help out constructively, no matter what the situation is.

## Ministering

Deep pleasure comes to the Christian who feels that he is going even a little distance in healing the hurt of another. When your act of ministering is over and you look back on it, you thank God for his grace in letting you experience this Christlike kind of joy. This enjoyment is cleansing for you; healing; inspiring. Since ministering is at the heart of what it means to be a Christian, enjoyment is bound to result.

This ministering can take place even in the classroom. As we shall see in chapter 3, you can minister significantly to the teacher during the study, as well as to fellow class members. And, of course, you can help to heal the minds and hearts of persons outside the class session, bringing joy to you which no other Christian experience can cause. As with the other types of enjoyment mentioned here, *there are* persons who experience this kind of joy. Be sure you are one of them!

## Studying the Bible

When was the last time you had the thrill of discovering an excellent book on your favorite subject?—The best book ever on how to play winning golf!—How to make your yard blossom like a garden!—Sure-fire ways to find and catch fish!—Winning at chess!

The Bible is universally acknowledged as being alive, timely, inspiring, and supremely practical—a "how-to-do-it" book for living in this life and the next. Enjoyment is applying your mind and heart strenuously to discovering God's will in his Word, and in doing that will.

## Making Progress

No doubt you have thought while reading these paragraphs: *I just don't enjoy Bible study in all these ways. I wish I did, but I don't.* All right. Let's add one more way that we enjoy, and see if it helps you. You will admit that it is fun to make progress, won't you? Whether it is becoming a more skilful fisherman, or gardener, or cook, or golfer, or chess player. It brings you pleasure to improve.

Making progress in Bible knowledge, understanding, convictions, and obedience to Christ also brings you pleasure. You are happy with your improvement in the ability to take part with others in Bible study. You feel good about growing in the capacity to *enjoy* more different ways of studying the Bible with others.

The apostle Paul thought that to press on toward the mark for the prize of the high calling of God in Christ Jesus was a thrilling experience. This is the course upon which you can be traveling as you continue this exploration of how to enjoy Bible study with others. The great violinist, Sarasate, was once called a genius by a famous critic. "Genius!" he snorted. "For thirty-seven years I've practiced fourteen hours a day, and now they call me a genius." Going further with this little book may not make you a genius in Bible discussion—though it could! But it certainly can help you develop an outlook and an approach in Bible study with others that will bring you deep spiritual joy.

# Chapter 2
## Getting Ready for Class

People who talk a lot become leaders in the group even if they don't know what they are talking about! This disturbing fact was uncovered by an experiment at the University of Tennessee. A study of group leadership revealed that students who monopolized discussions but who were seldom correct were selected as leaders ahead of quiet ones who were usually right. You may not aspire to become a leader in your Bible study group. But you *do* want to know what you are talking about when you speak, don't you?

Therefore, what are some good ways to prepare for engaging in Bible study with others? The ideas which follow have brought spiritual satisfaction to others. You may have your own way of carrying on individual Bible study and of getting ready for class study. Or you may do the things we are about to discuss, but in a different order. Fine. Take these few thoughts and improve upon them every way you can to

bring you the most spiritual enrichment and
enjoyment in Bible study.

## Pray for Enlightenment

At one time or another—and more than once,
likely—during your private Bible study, you ask
for divine guidance. You want inspiration and
enthusiasm. You want enlightenment and clear
thinking. You know that of all the things Christ
wants you to do, serious Bible study is near the
top of the list. This study, of course, will confer
its own benefit. (You may not get to Sunday
School next Sunday, after all.) You feel that
you can count surely on the Holy Spirit's guidance as you make your own personal Bible exploration, reflection, and other preparation. And
you have confidence that, once you have made
this kind of preparation, you will have opportunity to reflect some of the results of this holy
effort during the coming class session.

## Begin with Inductive Bible Study

"Inductive" Bible study means Bible study in
which you go right into the Scriptures and let
them say to you what Christ wills. The famous
preacher George Henry Jowett once took a reg-
ularly scheduled tour of Buckingham Palace in
London. He saw very little, really—just what
hurrying tourists usually see. In fact, he had
the feeling that he was not seeing the royal palace at all, but just what the guards and guides
wanted him to see.

Some years later, Jowett became the close

friend of a son of the royal family. When he then was invited to the palace, the ropes were down and locked doors were opened. He really saw the royal palace for the first time, for a royal family member was conducting him.

Through inductive Bible study you bypass, for the time, the usual "lesson" tour through Bible passages. The Holy Spirit is conducting you. Here you discover verse by verse what is really in the Bible for you.

For this first stage of Bible study, place before you only your notebook, your pencil, and your favorite Bible translations. You are going to God's Word with your own questions, allowing the Bible to reveal its truths. Make notes as you explore the Bible. Your Scripture passage may be a long one such as David's experiences in 2 Samuel, chapters 11–18; or parts of the Psalms; or the more sharply defined 2 Samuel 15:1–12 and 18:31–33.

Ask your own questions of the Scriptures. And you may want to add some of the following ones to your list in this stage of your individual Bible study:

(1) What does this passage teach about God? What words interpret or describe him? (List these words.)

(2) What words characterize or interpret the *believer?*

(3) What is a key word, phrase, or verse?

(4) Is there a *promise* here for me to claim?

(5) Which *commands* should I obey? (List these commands.)

(6) What *sins* or *mistakes* should I avoid?

(7) Is there an *example* here for me to follow?

(8) What *blessing* should I be enjoying?

(9) Is there something here that calls for *celebration? thanksgiving? praise?*

(10) Is God *convicting* me about something? Do I need to stop here and confess?

(11) Specifically, how can I *apply* these truths to my life today? Should this application change my relationships?

(12) Is there a *problem* in this passage that puzzles me? Do I need help in understanding it or interpreting it?

(13) Which verse would be good to *memorize?*

(14) Does there seem to be a natural division, theme, *outline,* or helpful thought pattern that makes understanding easier?

(15) What is a good *paraphrase* of this theme into my own language? (Write this out briefly.) Does this help me see the meaning clearer?

(16) Can a ballad or poem be *composed* including these ideas?

(17) Dare I form these concepts into an *affirmation* or covenant with God?

(18) What is a private, personal *prayer* for me based on these verses? (Phrase your prayer.)

(19) What is a *summary* or the essence of the passage?

(20) What reflective thoughts do I have on the passage? (Write these briefly.)

After this enriching Bible study-worship experience, you will want to make more specific preparation for Sunday.

## *Examine the Topic and Scripture*

Your custom may be to use a quarterly or booklet as your chief preparation resource material besides the Bible. Fine. Read and analyze your quarterly material. First ask: What is the topic for Sunday? Remember to ask yourself a little later whether the topic, as printed, accurately reflects the teaching of the passage. For you are studying the Bible, not topics. However, the topic often gives you a start in reading the passage with understanding. So you notice what is the stated quarterly theme of the passage.

The Scripture passages that we shall use for illustration in this specific preparation are 2 Samuel 15:1–12 and 18:31–33. The larger biblical background will include chapters 11–18. These are the passages which form the biblical framework for the companion volume to this book (for the teacher).* The Bible study topic may be something like "Developing More Loving Relationships in the Home."

Use two or three translations of the Bible in order to see better what the Scriptures really say. Get your note paper and pencil ready to write down any further questions or comments that come to you as you read. The way the Scriptures will speak to you will depend, of course, upon who you are (your age, your family situation, your attitudes toward many things, your personal problems and concerns).

* *Leading Dynamic Bible Study,* by Rice A. Pierce (Broadman Press, Nashville) 1969.

Jot down anything additional to which you want to give further thought. Especially include what you think you want to bring up in class that is related to this biblical account. It may be your own concerns that come out here. Or it could be the concerns that you know the teacher or certain fellow class members have.

If you are a young adult, no doubt you want class discussion to be fair in trying to understand Absalom's feelings. If you are an older adult, you may "bridge the gap" and feel concern about this same question. Or you may feel closer to the problem of David in his tragic relationship to Absalom. You can find many biblical questions to explore here, and many problems from life which the biblical account reflects. Write these thoughts down while they come to you in the inspiration of the moment.

## *Read Commentaries*

Your quarterly commentary or student's book can start you off after you read the Scripture passage itself. See if the writer reacted to the passage the same way you did. If he did, it will be a miracle! Underscore or bracket the writer's good points. Put a question mark beside statements you want the teacher and class to analyze with you.

Remember that space prevented your quarterly writer from saying all that he wanted to say. (His editor may have prevented a bit more!) And so the writer will be only too happy if what he wrote prompts you and the class to become modern-day Bereans and test his writing against the Scriptures.

But more thorough commentaries than your quarterly may be needed to satisfy some of your study interests. A Bible dictionary may even be pressed into service. For your quarterly is not likely to give the meaning of every difficult word, or the story of Absalom's early life. Nor may it have room to weigh the father-son problems which existed between the young man Absalom and David prior to the rebellion —unless this is the topic for Bible study. Use larger commentaries wisely.

A class member on one occasion was not satisfied with the interpretation which the writer of his personal study guide had given a certain verse. And he knew how certain class members would want to interpret the verse on Sunday morning. So he went to a "conservative" commentary first and found there the explanation which both satisfied him and would carry weight with these certain friends in the class. "If I had been trying to get a balanced interpretation from another viewpoint," he said later, "I would have gone first to a 'liberal' commentary and then moved around from there to a more conservative one."

Thus you see that the Bible passage guides your preparation for class study. Your personal problems and concerns enter in. The concerns which you know your teacher and other members have are bound to come into your thinking. And now we say that what you do before class time *concerning other persons* can affect your preparation significantly. For what you do in witnessing and ministering before Sunday can enrich your later class Bible study tremendously.

What interpretation of the power of love do you think the following woman could offer in class? She was a Quaker and, as such, did not believe in violence. She was wealthy. One night she came home late and found a burglar in her house searching for jewelry. When he turned on her with a gun in his hand, the woman said to him calmly: "Put your gun down. I hate guns. I promise I will not call the police after you have gone. Take what you need. I have more jewelry than I can ever use." The burglar stared in surprise: he had never been received in such a manner on a robbery. Then he ran from the house empty-handed. Days later there was a note in the woman's mailbox which read: "Madam, I have known nothing but hate and fear in my life. I can deal with these. But I was powerless in the face of your kindness."

Living out Christian convictions strengthened in private Bible study can help you experience that deep joy of being a doer for Christ, and not a reader only. And the person you touch may respond in faith or come for Bible study, himself. Then other roads to enjoyment and challenge open up to you and to him as a result of this "preparation for Sunday."

# Chapter 3
## *"Well, Here We Are . . ."*

In chapter 1 we saw that Bible study with others is something to be valued and enjoyed. We explored some ways that this kind of Bible study brings you satisfaction and pleasure of the deepest kind. Now we look at what *you* can do *in class* that will bring these kinds of enjoyment to you, to your teacher, and to fellow class members. Remember one thing, however: Even though you are planning to play a serious role in your coming classroom Bible study, you will still be just one of the members.

A college president once received a very candid response from the father of a hopeful applicant for admission. A question on the special form the president had sent read: "Outline the leadership capabilities of your daughter." The father wrote back: "My daughter has no leadership capabilities. But she is an intelligent follower."

The college president telephoned the father upon receipt of the remarkable reply and admitted the young woman immediately. "Of the thousands of applicants to our college," the president exclaimed, "this is the first girl who is not a natural-born leader. We need her!"

You are going to follow your teacher's lead in Bible study. As we go along, you will see that the word "follow" has a broad meaning for us. You will not be stifled and exasperated. But we *are* talking about helping your teacher and other class members discover their own joy, too, in Bible study.

## Be a Pray-er

The famed American scientist, Joseph Henry would prepare his experiments with meticulous care. Then he would go over the experiment several times in his head to smooth out every detail. When all was in readiness for the experiment, he would stop, raise his hand, and ask everyone to engage in silent prayer. "Why do you do this?" someone asked. "Because God is here," was the reply. God is certainly also present when people sincerely gather to search his Word for truths yet to be discovered for their lives.

Your prayer for the Holy Spirit's help is thus the first open doorway to enjoying Bible study with others. You pray for your own needy self —first as you prepare and then as you join in discussing what God's Word is saying to all of you. You pray that you will say things which help to make Bible study more serious and Christ-honoring.

You pray for your teacher as he seeks to be a good steward of his ministry through guiding class Bible study. And you pray for others in the class that their response will come from the heart. You ask God, in his providence, to work his healing upon confused and distressed class members through the means of serious, evangelistic Bible study.

This very ministry of prayer on your part brings cleansing, healing, and peace to you. And it brings God's promised blessing and joy to others.

## Be a Listener

Listening in class also is one of the first things you do to experience deep satisfaction in Bible study with others. You enjoy that blessed silence that we already have discussed. But listening is more than doing nothing! You can profit much and contribute much to the class just by listening.

You may listen in order to satisfy your own mental and emotional needs. For instance, you want to know what someone else is saying. So you look the speaker in the eye and perhaps jot down a key word occasionally as he speaks. Or you may listen to restore calm to your soul after already speaking perhaps too much. Or you are not sure what you want to say, so you remain silent a while. Also, there is a kind of listening that adds weight to the Bible interpretation you already have proposed to the class. Rather than beginning to argue, you remain silent and smiling. Then—if you were "right"—you enjoy seeing the discussion come around to your own feeling about the Bible truth being studied.

But you also can bring enjoyment to your *teacher* by listening. Did you ever have the good feeling of speaking to a group of people who seemed to hang on your every word? One of the finest ways of expressing appreciation to your teacher is to sit and listen closely to what he is saying. By various genuine (not overdone) expressions on your face, you can show that you are following him with interest. This kind of listening may not be easy for you. It often takes conscious effort—and practice—to offer this kind of appreciative listening and ministry to your teacher. But the rewards for both you and your teacher are worth the exercise in learning.

Good listening, then, is active and not passive response to the teacher. Since you do not need to pass judgment immediately upon the interpretations he is making, you are hearing him out. Time for verbal response will come later. Now you choose to listen.

When it comes to listening to fellow *class members,* you become even more a pleasure to others! A busy publisher sat quietly while a

forceful visitor outlined in great detail a pet project of his. Too many minutes later, the visitor
wound up his monologue by saying: "You're
talking to a man who . . ." The publisher smiled
and said: "But I haven't said a word, yet!"

You may be expected to listen respectfully to
the teacher. But now you are not only refrain-
ing from talking—but also listening with interest and animation—to a fellow class member as
he reveals his own theory about the lingering
love of David for the rebellious son. And it is
here that you show the highest honor toward
him. He knows that he is being heard. If you
later must disagree with him about what Absalom meant, or what God desired, you have
shown him love in carefully hearing your friend
out. Being disagreed with hurts far less than
not being heard.

Counselors have discovered that talking out
their problems merely into a tape recorder was
a big help to thirty juvenile delinquents. Inner
conflicts were released and healing began. As
one of the youths said: "It helped to get it out
of my system." If talking into a lifeless machine
can achieve such results, what may heart-to-
heart talk with concerned, listening fellow class
members accomplish?

## Be a Morale Builder

Did you ever try to be the morale builder at
home or at work? If you have done this, you
know that Sunday School classes also need

their spirits lifted at times. Maybe the teacher is discouraged. Or class members are saying: "What's happening to us? We're slowly dying."

Even your own feeling about the class may be low. At this point, after prayer and with the Holy Spirit's help, you do something. You screw up your courage and say something hopeful. Don't be like the old Vermont farmer who sat rocking on the porch one evening with his wife of fifty years beside him. "Molly, sometimes when I think what you have meant to me all these years, it's all I can do to keep from telling you." Don't wait. Speak up. Say something like: "I *need* this passage of Scripture we're studying today. It speaks to me!" Or maybe you compliment the teacher privately after class for his emphasis and suggest that he sound out the class about more concerned visitation.

If spirits are low or a slightly strained atmosphere prevails, use a little natural humor: "Bill, I believe you've been talking to my wife about me. You just now hit me between the eyes!" And laugh when you say this! Or at some appropriate place in class discussion, you show keen interest and say: "This sounds good. And I would feel better about our conclusion if we would *do* something specific about this Bible study in terms of some witness or ministry." Then you offer help toward *setting some goal* that Christ once gave his followers. This raising of members' spiritual sights to attempt something compassionate in Christ's name will foster self-respect and raise the morale of the class. And it can help *your* experience of Bible study again to become liberating, cleansing, satisfying. Your own morale is lifted. For you again have become a part of doing Christ's will, and not of hearing only.

But what if you didn't think of anything to say? What if you drifted around in boredom and depression with everybody else in the class? It was someone else who lifted the sights of members to Christ and his mission. You still can become a morale builder. You immediately sense the inspiration of the idea. You give quick support. You show enthusiasm. Enthusiasm has a root meaning of being "god-possessed." So you become truly possessed of God to add vitality to an idea which can cause your Bible class to rise from its lethargy and honor Christ. Again, you find enjoyment in this support of another in Bible study.

In still another way, you can find joy in your Sunday School class experience through being a morale builder. You can remember what it means to be appreciated. Maybe that member who made the suggestion in class that saved the day hasn't been too fortunate lately in his attempts to be helpful. So you go to him after class and express appreciation for what he did. Or maybe the teacher made a sincere attempt to teach better, to secure more thought and honest response to God's Word in class. He needs encouragement in his faltering first attempt. You build him up tremendously by a kind word of appreciation after class for the "stimulating time we had today in Bible study." And truly the class can only get better with more and better experiences like that one.

Maybe a certain class member has been absent often lately. You speak to him after class, expressing some word of genuine appreciation for what he is or for some act of ministry which you know he has rendered. Such a genuine ministering to one who well may feel that he doesn't matter to the class can draw him more closely into the fellowship of the Bible study group. And your heart is doubly warmed by the experience.

### Be an Idea Man

Closely related to the humble enjoyment of being a morale builder in the class—but different—is that of being an idea man. You are one who helps members come up with ideas that can become solutions to spiritual problems in their Bible study. Your teacher has just pointed out the difficulty of understanding what David's responsibility was in the breakdown of relationships with his son Absalom. Or the "problem" simply may be a Bible content one like what was the family background of Absalom—his mother, his probable early life, and so on. Your teacher may be trying, on the other hand, to help the class discover or examine their convictions about how David should have dealt with

Absalom before the rebellion. Or you, the teacher, and the class may be trying to decide what a
young father can do now with his small son. He
wants to feel that, later in a crisis, he may have
a better chance than David had when Absalom
was about to rebel.

You will experience a deep satisfaction as you
draw upon your own preparation, experience,
and insight to help the class over this kind of
Bible study hurdle. Maybe your Saturday night
research turned up the interesting fact that
Absalom's mother was a pagan princess. And
you offer this information when the stage of
class discussion makes this information shed
helpful light on the Bible point being studied.
Or you may have a small son and you have
been wrestling with the very question of how to
build paths of communication between a father
and a young son. You share with the class your
experience in trying, with God's help, to think
through this problem.

Or you may know that a friend in the class is
struggling with the problem of a rebellious
teen-age son. He has not sought your counsel,
and you do not intrude inappropriately into his
personal life here. But since the Bible study is
on this subject, you enter the discussion and
offer the best insight that the Holy Spirit can
give to a concerned, Bible-believing friend (you)
about what David might have done. You can
trust the Holy Spirit to take the idea which you
have offered and use it in the healing ministry

which you humbly and discreetly have attempted within the circle of class Bible study.

You can see that playing the role of idea man at times in the Bible study has unlimited possibilities. It can relate to other roles that you may take up as circumstances seem to call for them. You may come up with a reconciling interpretation of the passage when differences seem to become disturbing to group fellowship. You may suggest a goal for the remaining study time when circumstances seem to be giving the teacher difficulty. You may offer a plan of action when the class wants to do something during the week in obedience to God's Word but cannot come up with a practical idea.

You can say later, after making such a contribution as we have been discussing: "I enjoyed the class this morning." And your teacher may call you blessed!

## Be a Reconciler

If God has blessed you with adaptability, you will enjoy taking the part of reconciler at times in the class. It is a good feeling—when experienced with appropriate humility—to be able to see both sides of a question in the Bible discussion and to help reconcile conflicting views.

God's Word is not self-contradictory. And so any successful effort at helping teacher and class work through differences of interpretation to a constructive conclusion will bring pleasure. No one is more appreciated in a Sunday School class than one who has prepared well enough for Sunday to help get over problems of detailed Bible facts. Even the teacher usually will be relaxed and sure enough of his position in the class to welcome your help when some specific bit of Bible knowledge is needed to clear up a point. (Of course, you will resist the temptation to become a know-it-all. See chap. 8.) Nor is anyone appreciated more in the class than the one who can—and will—help interpret the position of a member who is having difficulty expressing how he really feels about a Bible truth.

Sometimes good and committed class members are ready to act upon God's Word, but are about to fall out over what to do. You can help. A situation like this existed in colonial days during the Constitutional Convention. Then one of the least pious of the founding fathers became a reconciler. Benjamin Franklin called the assembly to prayer. "God governs in the affairs of men," he said. "And if a sparrow cannot fall without his notice, is it probable that an empire can rise without his aid?"

A lively discussion about Bible meanings easily can become a matter of spiritual "life and death" to an overzealous class member. It is easy to "get out on a limb" and need help getting back. A member of the British Parliament once had been slandered by a political opponent. A fellow M.P. suggested that it would be "manly" to officially resent the insult. The slandered man replied: "Perhaps. But wouldn't it be Godlike to forgive?" As reconciler, you can help fellow class members get over rough spots in personal relationships when they arise in the midst of serious Bible discussion.

Perhaps you do not need convincing further about the joy of playing the role of reconciler in Bible study with others. Did not our Lord say: "Happy are those who work for peace among men" (TEV)?.

## Be a Testifyer

One of the deepest joys of the Christian is to express to congenial friends how he feels about things spiritual. Your Sunday School class offers this opportunity in a unique way. For the teacher and class are discussing these very ideas and feelings during Bible study. What more natural thing is there for you to do than select the appropriate place and express how you feel about them, too?

Of course, you can testify about anything from how hard it was to understand 2 Samuel 14:24 last night—to what Christ means in your life—to what a thrill you had in visiting a new resident in the neighborhood for Christ and the class. When discussing David's grief over Absalom's death, you can tell in a discreet way—if you feel it would be helpful—how Christ has helped you over distressing places in your family experiences. You can express what Jesus has meant to you in your personal life—how far *you* would have been by now along David's road of adultery and murder if Christ had not given you the strength to be different from what you might have been.

You can see that this kind of response in Bible study comes from utter humility and modesty and genuine gratitude to God. We are talking about taking an honest part in class discussion, one which cleanses and liberates you and reassures and spiritually enlightens others. You may discover after the class is over that you reinforced a fellow class member tremendously. You said what he could not yet bring himself to say to others about God's forgiveness and cleansing. And your teacher will value your response highly. For you urged spiritual thoughts from your chair in the class which he would have had to exhort from "up there" as teacher, if he had expressed them.

The statement just made does not mean that you do not respect and accept a genuine testimony from the teacher. It simply means that sometimes, with some class members, a testimony from someone sitting next to them carries more weight than one from the teacher who is "supposed" to say such things.

If one of the deepest joys is to be heard by others and still be accepted and appreciated, then testifying in Bible study can bring you keen enjoyment. For in no other way, except *acting* how you feel, can you better reveal yourself. You experience the genuineness of bringing closer into line for others how you *seem* to be and how you *are*.

# CHAPTER 4
## Coming to Grips

The thoughts and feelings of each "unpromising" person in the class deserves your support in Bible study. Years ago a Kansas City editor turned away a young artist because his sketches showed he obviously had no talent. The young man rented a mice-infested garage and turned out sketches for publicity jobs that local churches gave him. Finally his work began to catch on, and so did his famous Mickey Mouse.

### Be a Reinforcer

Every class member may not be a budding "Walt Disney" of philosophy and Bible interpretation. Your teacher may not be a famous discussion leader. But the results of your quiet and steady support of these persons as class discussion goes on can surprise you.

You well may ask, however: *What pleasure will I get out of "reinforcing" other persons during Bible study? What does reinforcing another person mean, anyway?*

This strange word simply means *helping* other persons in the class, including the teacher. Do you believe that your teacher wants your help? He certainly does. For what goes on in the minds and hearts of your class members determines your teacher's "success" in leading Bible study. And the satisfaction which all of you get from Sunday School depends upon the degree of seriousness and enthusiasm with which you enter into your Bible study together.

You can reinforce your teacher in many ways. From your preparation, you can support his statements of biblical fact (when he is right). He does not want to be regarded as an oracle who can never be wrong, who looks down on his members as he "teaches." But he does want support of a factual nature when you can give it. Often you have time to scan the Scripture passage while he is discussing it. At a certain point he needs a Scripture reference. So he says: "Which verse is it that describes David's anguish?" You have it ready to give so that discussion can move on smoothly.

You can see from this simple example that if you can go further at another time during the class and express your own *conviction* in support of the teacher's interpretation or application of a passage, you help him even more. When the teacher is suggesting that the way David's wives lived in separate quarters limited his opportunity to influence his sons aright, some members may take issue with this

"soft-pedaling" of David's responsibility. It is
here that you can come in with something like:
"Well, I know from experience that a father can
go just so far in determining how a young
adult son will act."

When the teacher is faced with interpreting a
Bible passage that speaks a little too plainly for
the views of some strong-minded members, you
can reinforce him (and God's Word). The very
fact that you feel, deep down, a little bit as
these fellow members of yours feel only increases your ability to support a teacher who is
trying to be faithful to Christ's commands.

One day Charles Evans Hughes, later to become chief justice of the Supreme Court,
walked down the aisle to join Calvary Baptist
Church in Washington, D.C. With Mr. Hughes
that morning stood a young Chinese college
student and a washerwoman, also applying for
membership. The pastor, with deep spiritual
perception, commented to his people: "My
friends, I will have you notice that at the cross
of Christ the ground is level."

The ground also is level in the kind of Sunday School class we are talking about. Each
person speaks and his views are heard for their
worth. And you can help keep this ground level.

But when it comes to reinforcing a fellow
class member who is finding the going rough in
discussion, your task may become more difficult
than it was in supporting the teacher. You still
can say something like this, however: "I haven't

thought through everything that Bill has said, but I *do* believe what he said about father loving son no matter what has happened."

Your neighbor in the class does not need to be hard pressed in biblical interpretation before you can support him, however. He may be one of those in the group who is hesitant to speak. But now he speaks. And suddenly you sense a few seconds of deadly silence settling around his offering to the class. So you quickly pick up his thought with, "Yes, Hank has made a point that opens up an important question . . ." If you believe that the Holy Spirit truly is in the midst of such serious Bible study, you will find him helping you go on to discover something of the real concern that prompted Hank's response. You may not come up with exactly what Hank felt. Then, perhaps a "Hank, spell out a little more what you mean" will bring a new experience for Hank of coming outside himself in the light of biblical truth.

If you want to support others in their willingness to open up their hearts in Bible study, the opportunities and joys are unlimited. Vary your assistance from information to questions to opinions to proof to testimony. Every phase of Bible study with others needs what you can offer as a reinforcer.

## *Be a Thinker*

A cartoon once showed a pitiful mother with her destitute children about her, listening to the pious pronouncements of a "religious man."

The caption under the picture had the mother saying: "Father, forgive him. He knows not what he is talking about."

To give the kind of verbal support in the Sunday School class that we have been discussing does require awareness. It means that you do some thinking during the Bible study. We have already talked about listening. When you think, you listen; you let others talk, you reflect. But don't think and remain silent so long, of course, that all the ideas come in and a conclusion is reached before you even speak.

You, your teacher, and other class members owe it to each other—and to Christ—to bring your best thinking to bear on what the Bible says to all of you from Sunday to Sunday. The apostle Paul said that Christ's word is to live in your heart as you "teach and instruct each other with all wisdom" (Col. 3:16, TEV). The "wisdom" comes from prior Bible study, prayer, reflection, and experience. And it comes from listening to what your teacher and others are saying, then applying your best thought to it.

You don't want to come to class with your mind made up on every Bible interpretation and application, of course. But you do want to come with some thoughtfully arrived-at, *tentative* ideas and conclusions. And lest this sound like it would be unheard of to come to Bible study without this kind of thoughtful preparation, let us admit right here that such a thing is heard of.

What kind of thinking do you do as you

study the Bible with others? For one thing, you may sense that all the discussion about what the Bible says and means has dealt in generalities. It's been what "they" ought to do, what "people" say, and what isn't "right." So you ask the speaker: "Who is they?" "What people?" "What do you mean by 'right'?" "Why isn't it right?" Your teacher will appreciate it deeply that someone in the class is following his comments and discussion closely enough—and with enough concern—to ask for a clearer statement.

Or maybe you are listening to a member next to you and you are moved to say: "As I think this idea out to what seems to be its logical conclusion, Absalom's only chance of ever making a strong claim to the throne was to do what he did. Is this what you are saying? Is this a young man's best response to a 'stone wall'?"

You also play the role of thinker in a satisfying way when you ask other class members to consider carefully, for instance, the practical effect of a ministry they are planning as a result of their Bible study. Your reaction to the proposal outlined on the chalkboard may be: "The idea certainly expresses the concern we all have agreed that we have. But will the plan work out well for the parents in the family? Can we improve this plan?"

You play the valued role of thinker whenever you call, in a kind and relaxed way, for a closer look at the Bible and at opinions that are being expressed. Or when you put your mental weight behind the tackling of a biblical problem that needs solving. Or when you sit and reflect, and then speak, so as to help teacher and class members out of some biblical dilemma facing them. And the pleasure is not all yours when you succeed! (Not to mention the happiness for you at seeing yet another endeavor that is carried on in the name of Christ come to life and bear fruit.)

## Be an Inquirer

When you become an inquirer in the Sunday School class, in a sense you may be giving expression to the thinking that you have been doing. Yet there is something different about this role; anybody can do it. Billy Sunday was not just anybody, but he did raise the kind of inquiring on one occasion which could occur to anyone who is listening to classroom discussion. The question for discussion on that occasion was whether joining the church makes one a Christian. Billy Sunday's question, to get his point over, was whether walking into a garage makes one an automobile. We'll admit that a little thinking went along with Mr. Sunday's response!

You do not need to be a deep thinker to be an inquirer. You are just interested. Some rather "simple" minds can come up with some mighty good questions during Bible study. For they express a felt need for understanding. You can become appreciated by others in the class even with an inquiry like: "Frank, I just don't get what you are saying about Joab's intentions toward Absalom." You see, courage and interest are the two possibly most distinguishing characteristics of the inquirer: courage to admit you don't know or understand something, and interest enough to want to understand. And you can add another dimension to this role in Bible study with others: a sense of joint responsibility with the teacher for members' being able to understand what is being said. If understanding is not there, Bible study becomes a ceremony, an act, a farce.

You can add life to the Bible study experience for everyone with a simple question to the teacher like: "Mary, do you know who Absalom's mother was? I've never thought about this side of Absalom's story." Or a question like this to a class member can add genuine interest and motivation: "Sue, that's an interesting theory about Absalom's early life. Where did you get it?" (You hope that it was not given in the class member's study aids for this Bible passage, and you missed it!) You may discover a valuable new resource book with this inquiry. And you certainly confirm Sue in her appreciation for this extra Bible study aid that she has used.

You can see that we are dealing here with the inquiring approach to strengthening Bible study. You are asking for clarity, for facts, for basic thinking. It is easy for the teacher to make inaccurate statements when leading a lively class in Bible study! So you ask your teacher: "Helen, did you mean to say . . .?" Or to a fellow class member you say, during the warm give-and-take of discussion: "Sam, you said . . . , but do you really mean this?" You are simply asking, you are not telling or rebuking. Nor are you debating. Your motivation is interest. It is curiosity. It is fairness. It is helpfulness and purposefulness in Bible study. You can go too far with this role in the class, of course. We shall discuss this in chapter 8.

The enjoyment you experience with this role is having your desire for understanding satisfied. It is the good feeling of helping someone express himself accurately and thus become understood better. It is the Word of God being examined with interest and accuracy. It is Christ's wishes looked at squarely and responded to.

## Be a Door Opener

A sign at a research laboratory in Washington, D.C., was observed to read: "Consider the turtle—he doesn't make any progress unless he sticks his neck out." Or recall the proverbial farmer who replied to all questions about his crops: "Didn't plant nothing. Just played it safe." And so another role you may play in helping Bible study become more stimulating for you and the class involves sticking your neck out—participating "dangerously." You go beyond just inquiring. You do need the courage of the inquirer to speak up. But you need even more courage than the inquirer. You will not be just playing it safe.

You may feel that a ticklish subject just cannot be ignored if Christ's words in the Sermon on the Mount are to speak clearly to you and the class. Or you may know that your teacher is having an agonizing time with his teen-age son. He will find it very hard to dig into the dynamics of the God-David-Absalom relationship where you feel you and the class want to go for honest Bible study. So you open the door to this question when it seems that time or circumstance is going to pass it by. Again, you approach prayerfully doing this sort of thing even though you do feel led of God to open up the subject. (More about the cautions later.)

Perhaps you have seen those rare times in a class when the door to discussion is not open. Then you must be quite resourceful if you get to express a thought or feeling. Maybe it has never occurred to the teacher that any of you would have anything to say, or would want to say it. Your teacher, on the *most* rare of occasions, might even assume that some special situation would cause everyone to remain silent. But, Spirit led, you cannot remain silent. You must open the door. You do not mean to crash into the proverbial china shop. You do not mean to be rude. But you do want to testify, to give expression during this Bible study to what Christ has put on your heart.

But your teacher does not stop. He does not look up from his notes. He keeps talking (or reading). What will you do? You, of course, will not interrupt him in the middle of a sentence. For a few seconds you silently play the role of thinker. You realize that your teacher is human and, therefore, must *breathe.* So you mentally sharpen up what you want to say—and wait for your opportunity. You wait for a statement that has a bearing on what is on your own heart, a statement from the teacher that can open the door to your response. Then, at the end of that statement, *when he stops to breathe,* you say quietly: "Joe, about what you have just said—do you think it is possible that God meant . . . ?"

You have opened the door to class discussion. If other class members have convictions that are hurting to be said, this is their chance, too. It just could be that never again in the class will you have to screw up your courage and lie in wait for an opportunity to speak what Christ has put on your heart.

Your role as door opener does not always have to require such courageous effort, however. An open, accepting atmosphere already may prevail in the class because of your teacher. It is not a matter of getting a chance to speak, but of noticing how the Bible study is going—and not going. How the class discussion is going may be a matter of personalities, Bible content, or procedure. You can open the door to a *per-*

*son* simply by concluding your own response with: "But I'd like to know how Sally feels about this. She works with people like this a lot." You can open the door to *another side of the Bible truth* by answering your teacher's question with: "Yes, I do think you have pointed out an important factor in David's record as a father. Which leads, I think, into another question: Where did David get his ability to repent so fully and ask for God's cleansing?"

As for opening the door to *procedure,* remember what we have just said about helping discussion take place where there was none before. Also, your teacher may welcome as a gift from heaven a suggestion from you like: "We seem to be disagreed about what this passage is really saying. Why don't we all read the verses silently for a moment, then say how we understand them?" You are introducing the class to Bible research, reflection, and response. Or you may even say: "Frank, you are trying to get us to say what this passage means to us. But no one will speak first. How about starting over here with Dan and just go around the room?" You have opened the door for the class to use circular response in Bible study.

You can open the door to participation by the whole class—set a tone of cooperative response for the teacher's reassurance—by reacting early in the session to the teacher's first invitation to speak up. It is better for two or three of you immediately to show yourselves eager to voice your thinking than for all of you to hang back "in honor preferring one another." Courtesy and kindness can be shown later, and in other ways. The teacher can referee.

Playing this role of door opener in Bible study with others can cause you to feel a deep gratitude to Christ. For he has used you to help make Bible study more exciting, more thorough, and more inclusive of every member. But you can go even farther with this role, and with the best of spiritual intentions. We shall look into this further role in the next chapter.

## CHAPTER 5

# *"So What?"*

Omit this brief section if you wish. But if you will stay with it, you can rest assured you will not be reading about helping the devil in his work! In fact, your only motivation for being the "devil's advocate" in Bible study is to stimulate your fellow members to do more serious thinking about what God is saying through the Bible.

## *The Devil's Advocate*

Suppose you and your Bible class are studying the ministry of Paul as described in Acts. Would you seriously reject Paul's methods and call him a troublemaker—just for a while for the sake of challenging careful thought? Perhaps you have seen the following imaginary letter to the Apostle Paul, who had applied to a missionary board for work as a traveling preacher:

"Dear Mr. Paul: We recently received an application from you for service under our board. It is our policy to be frank and as open-minded as possible with all our applicants.

"We are told that you are afflicted with severe eye trouble. This is certain to be an insuperable handicap to an effective ministry. Our board requires 20–20 vision among its pastors.

"At Antioch we learn you opposed Dr. Simon Peter, an esteemed denominational leader, and actually rebuked him publicly. You stirred up so much trouble that a special board meeting had to be convened at Jerusalem.

"We hear that you are making tents on the side.

"Is it true that you have a jail record? Certain brethren report that you did two years at Caesarea and were imprisoned in Rome.

"It hurts me to tell you, Brother Paul, but in all my experience I have never met a man so opposite to the requirements of our Foreign Mission Board."

In general, therefore, as devil's advocate this is what you do: You favor an unpopular interpretation or application of Bible truth *for a while*. Or you support a viewpoint that has been completely neglected. You may play this role two or three ways.

If your teacher is of an open, relaxed, nondefensive temperament, you may respond to her rather routine question like this: "Stephanie, I know you may expect someone to say that Absalom and his mother were all wrong. But *I'm* saying that when David forced Maachah to become his wife for reasons other than genuine affection, he nevertheless created a debt to her and her son by him . . . Furthermore, . . ." You push this position as far as you can logically do so. You are not trying to give the teacher trouble, or mess up the class atmosphere. You are dedicated to aiding a *thoughtful* study of how God works with an imperfect father who erred even as today's fathers and mothers err, but who clung to his God as many of today's parents are doing. Sometimes your class members will not come to grips with the bedrock meanings and important distinctions in the Scriptures unless they are prompted to do so when forced to disprove an outlandish interpretation. Of course, your class may not need to have its thought and response patterns shaken up this way.

You may play the devil's advocate to "smoke out" some of your usually silent class members. Some men and women will not speak up in Sunday School unless thoroughly aroused. Of course, you must express your views with all earnestness. Otherwise, members will see that you do not go all the way in your support of this particular biblical interpretation and may just be amused at you. But if one of these non-participating members comes alive and starts thinking, feeling, and testifying about the real meaning of God's Word, your friendly role will be well worth the effort.

Do not be afraid of appearing for the moment

to be wrong—of being on the unpopular side. In fact, do not ever fear being "wrong" when taking any kind of sincere part in Bible study. You are not proud, but humble. You do not know it all, but you *are* a learner. You have your self-respect. Also have a little spunk! Oliver Wendell Holmes once attended a conference in which he was the shortest man present. "Doctor Holmes," quipped a friend, "I should think you'd feel rather small among us big fellows." "I do," retorted Holmes. "I feel like a dime among a lot of pennies!"

In Bible study, you say what you think and feel. When you learn more you may change your views. But who says you are wrong, anyway? The Holy Spirit is speaking to you as well as to the teacher and to other class members. Priesthood of all believers means what it says. You have something to offer in Bible study with others, and you may be right!

## Be a Protector

Acting as protector in the class could have been discussed when we were thinking of a reconciling role, perhaps. But the problem is that sometimes you have a problem member in the class—or even a problem teacher. Just reconciling doesn't seem to do any good. You want to help achieve unity of the Spirit in the bond of peace, as the Apostle Paul said. But this member just doesn't respond favorably to gentle handling by the teacher or by any other class member.

You may need to protect your teacher's time. Yesterday's football game was *so* exciting! But time is valuable. Napoleon had a veritable passion for guarding his time. His motto was "Time is everything." Once he said: "I may lose battles, but no one will ever see me lose minutes." Whether Napoleon ever fell from his ideal on occasions, we won't explore. But at times you will have to say: "I liked the game, too. But I also want to know what we are going to do with 2 Samuel 15:12."

Or a class member may begin to dominate the discussion; or turn every seeming response to a Bible question into an attack on "those people in Washington"; or insist on quoting one questionable source all the time; or oversimplify every Bible truth that could yield itself to real spiritual probing; or turn every response into a criticism of the pastor; or even browbeat other members with his tenacity and dogmatic manner. Not to mention never staying on the subject when he says something, or blocking what others propose. What a class member! But maybe you can help the situation.

There may not be much enjoyment in playing this role of protector in the Sunday School class. And you may not often be called upon to help out in this way. But the point is that you can give needed aid to the teacher in the difficult situations just mentioned.

If a member just seems bent on doing all the talking, your teacher will know some ground rules like circular response which may help. If not, you and other members can move in kindly and largely fill up the speaking time the teacher offers to the class. Just don't let this friend seize the floor every time. Or you can say: "Id like to hear from Bill and Henry on this, too. We are discussing Absalom, and they have had some experience with juvenile boys."

When the same one always seems to want to block what the class is about to do as a result of Bible study, he may just want attention. As fellow class members (so that the teacher won't have to be "policeman" all the time), some of you press him for his reasons: "Ed, why won't this work?" "Don't you think the family needs help?" "What is a better way to help?" Pretty soon, Ed's objections may have melted away under the warm spotlight of persistent attention.

The member may have some obsession. He may be passionately opposed to the federal party in power, and explains the meaning of every utterance of Jesus in terms of "the rascals in Washington." Pass loosely over his comments. If your teacher asks for responses on a biblical interpretation and Jack comes out with his political viewpoint, you respond directly to the teacher's question just as if Jack had not spoken. You do not feel happy having to assist your teacher and the class in this manner. But

maybe it must be done. Better to try helping a
member become more constructive in Bible
study than to sit back and see God's holy hour
for Bible study largely lost because of such dis-
traction. And Jack well could get the hint from
such an approach. He may not realize the nature of his effect on the Bible study, and probably does not have such a thin skin that he is
easily offended. There is one thing to remember,
however: Jack is a Christian brother who needs
the ministry of the class. Running him off will
defeat the whole purpose of the outreaching
love of Christ.

The dynamic, saloon-shattering Carrie Nation felt that she knew more about preaching
than her preacher-husband. She chose his texts
for him, and often wrote his sermons. As general protector of all, she would sit in the front
row and coach him in audible tones as he tried
to inspire his little flock. When she thought he
had preached long enough, she would step into
the aisle and say in a loud voice: "That will be
all for today, David." Very seldom do you feel
the need to protect the class from your teacher.
And never in the manner of a Carrie Nation.
Even thinking of such a thing is disturbing. But
a teacher can become obsessed with one-sided
biblical interpretations, too; and tedious, unprofitable background facts; and political view-
points; and the love of hearing himself talk.
To protect the value and honor of God's living
truth in the sight of the class and any visitors

who may be present, once in a great while you may need gently to lead the teacher "back to the Bible." Without any direct reference to the biblically irrelevant or spiritually unprofitable statements your teacher has made, you can say: "Yes, that's a problem, but what about verse 4? Did David really . . . ?" The satisfaction that comes to you in serving as protector on rare occasions in the class can be in terms of the appreciation which your teacher and other class members feel for you. Not every person will feel able to play this role. And some situations just may not lend themselves to such redemptive effort. Some cautions, which no doubt you already have thought of, will be discussed in chapter 8. If you can see the need for responding as we have described here, in gentleness and with the best of motivations, perhaps you can feel good about having reclaimed the class time for genuine Bible study.

## Be an Analyst

An American in a Korean prison camp was among fifty captives from the United States. A Communist propagandist denounced Americans as a barbarous race whose latest atrocity was germ warfare. He produced a small insect. He said it was unspeakably deadly, one of millions dropped by American planes. He passed it around on a piece of paper. One prisoner on the front row picked up the insect, examined it carefully, and then, to the speaker's horror, popped it into his mouth. Everyone waited tensely for something to happen to the soldier. Nothing did. There were no more lectures on germ warfare.

You are an analyst in classroom Bible study when you say to yourself things like this: *Has what we have said really been accurate and serious? And our time is about gone. Have we really gotten to the heart of this Bible passage? What still needs to be brought up?* Or you wonder if you feel good about how class discussion has gone: its mood, its balance, its inclusiveness. You are not assuming for yourself the teacher's role. But you are thinking like the mature, concerned class member that your teacher wants you to be.

The teacher of a lively Sunday School class is mentally and emotionally occupied in many directions. He can miss some things. You are free to sit in the corner and reflect on a verse of Scripture. Or on how Jim, next to you, was cut off in the discussion a minute ago. He was hurt. Other people do not know Jim like you do. So you seize a good opening and say: "Jim was making a point about David's career a minute ago, and I missed what he really meant to say. Jim, could you repeat what you said?" You play a valuable role in the class when you analyze—or simply, through awareness, make a mental note—of what happens in the class and then offer comments which are meant to help the situation.

You also can observe how your teacher reacted at a certain point in the study. He, too,
may need a little support during the discussion
or perhaps after class.

Or say you are silently reviewing the Bible
interpretations that have taken place. So you
may say: "Before we leave, shouldn't we see
what we think about the way David felt upon
hearing of Absalom's death? I mean, what all
went into David's grief and tears, do you
think?"

A small boy saw a jar of coins near the cash
register as he and his mother were leaving the
grocery store. "I want to give some money to
the poor children," he exclaimed. Soon the two
left the store, the boy happily unwrapping a
candy bar his mother had bought him as a re-
ward for his generous impulse—with her money.
At that moment a neighbor boy stopped and
asked his little friend: "Can I have a piece of
your candy?" "No," snarled the boy. "Go buy
your own candy." You may size up whether the
class really means what they have been talking
about, whether they apparently are going to try
doing something about what everyone has been
discussing. Or will it just be "sit and talk about
the Bible"? You're just thinking, at this point;
analyze what is happening.

No doubt, also, you will want to analyze your
own part in the Bible study that has taken
place. This matter will be discussed more fully
in chapter 8. But you will enjoy Bible study

with others more if you not only participate in
many ways but also reflect upon the experience.
Thus can the Holy Spirit go on beyond the actual experience of Bible discussion to give you
insights into what has happened spiritually to
you and the class.

## Be a Doer

You cannot take part in Bible study with
others the way we have discussed it without
coming eventually to God's truth as found in
James 1:22: "Be ye doers of the word, and not
hearers only." Being a responsible person is
what James is talking about. For you cannot
really enjoy the study of God's Word unless
you feel that you are being honest about it.
Deep down you feel, after discussing Christ's
teaching, that you want to make a sincere effort
to obey him.

This desire for genuineness in Bible study
prompts you to go beyond analyzing what the
class has said about witnessing and ministering.
You do not speak now as a mere observer of
class progress, but as a doer: "This passage is so
strong on compassion and ministering. I feel
that we should follow through on Ed's idea of
seeing what we can do to help this father win
back his teen-age son." Or, "How would it be
for us to ask the women in our church missions
group to help us with this. Some of us are members of this group." Or, "Mary has said that it's

a pity the way this girl is neglected. I'll volunteer to do . . . if two or three others will help."

Your teacher may be gently hinting that some class members may be absent because they don't feel especially wanted in the group. You muster your courage, say no to that extra golf game, and reply to the teacher: "Sam, I'll visit two of these men between now and next Sunday if somebody here will go with me." You know, yourself, how just one "doer" in a class can get things rolling if the practical expression of concern has grown naturally out of the Bible study. And you also know that the thrill of looking back on a night of rewarding visits in the name of Christ exceeds the thrill even of a hole in one.

Most of the satisfying doing that we have discussed so far has begun in the class by your speaking up. But you discover an inner warmth by quietly making your own *personal* response to what God has said to you through his Word. You may go up to a class member after class and express appreciation for his testimony. You may tell a seldom-attending member how very glad you are to see her. You may tell her quite genuinely how much her presence means to the quality of Bible discussion in the class.

You may tell your teacher how glad you are that he opened up for discussion the biblical application that your class needed to face up to. You may thank him for his Christian restraint during a difficult point in the Bible study.

All of your outward response after class is not limited to talking, of course. You quietly go and visit the father who is distressed over his drug-ridden son. You offer simple concern; solid counsel, if he requests it; practical help. Or you ask Helen and your teacher to go with you to see what you three women can do for the mother in his family. You let the mother in another family know that she is not all alone in the world with her two small daughters, trying to hold a family together with an alcoholic husband.

Actually, doing the word of Christ is an essential outcome of truly studying the Bible with others. Without the doing, learning never takes place. Just as well to sit and listen; get up and walk out; come back next Sunday; sit and listen . . . But learning of Christ's love through doing—this brings the deepest joy.

CHAPTER 6

# *Special Ways to Participate*

We have been thinking about different ways to participate as you study the Bible with others. Other class members are taking part in one or more of these ways, too. All together, you join the teacher in a complete experience of Bible study.

In chapters 3, 4, and 5 we did not have in mind any particular teaching approach. We just assumed that you and other class members were encouraged by your teacher to explore and think seriously about God's Word, and to express and follow through on what you felt. Perhaps your teacher's favorite method of leading Bible study is lecture forum. Or it may be informal discussion (teaching through the use of probing questions). What we have discussed in previous chapters applies well to the situation you find yourself in when your teacher is using these two basic ways of teaching. Thus we may deal lightly at times later in this chapter with how you respond in these two Bible study situations and similar ones.

Not long ago a group of professional educators were gathered to do some creative planning. The leader of the group began the session in quite a nondirect way. His procedure was to come in, sit down in the circle, and assume a meditative pose. After a silent eternity of two or three minutes, one really quite capable young woman plaintively exclaimed: "I don't even know what I'm supposed to be thinking about!"

We are not about to go into those inscrutable group processes which some people erroneously think exist for their own sake and have little teaching value. But in the next two chapters, this book will fulfil its role as a companion volume to *Leading Dynamic Bible Study*. For that book was written to help the teacher who wants to move from pure lecture to an approach which allows class members to become active partners in studying God's Word. The book you are now reading was written to help you respond in a satisfying way when your teacher is leading this kind of Bible study which invites you to become a partner in learning.

In this chapter, then, we shall discuss how you may gain the most enjoyment and spiritual profit from your responses as your teacher uses *basic* teaching methods such as lecture forum, team-teaching forum, colloquy, informal discussion, and so on. Our sequence usually will follow the order of Bible study procedures found in *Leading Dynamic Bible Study*. Then we shall examine briefly in chapter 7 your responses in what are referred to in the teacher's book as *feature forums* and on pages 43–45 as *supplementary* Bible study approaches.

## The Lecture Forum

Very likely your teacher lectures often. For lecturing is a respected and often interesting way of teaching. You will notice, moreover, that the heading for this brief section refers to "lecture forum." "Forum" means that we assume your teacher will give you and other class members a chance to express your thoughts and feelings about what he says the Bible means. The preparation you made deserves a chance to be shared with the class. And so here are some things to do in order to respond well to your Sunday School teacher's leadership when he uses lecture forum. This way of leading Bible study is widely used. So it is the method dealt with first.

Picture the situation. You and the class are sitting quietly as the teacher begins to speak. As in every other role you play in Bible study with others, pray for your teacher and for the results of this Bible study experience. Then listen. Listen in all those supportive ways we discussed in chapter 3, plus several others that will occur to you depending upon what the teacher says.

Now the teacher has finished speaking. (He may have planned to lecture briefly, discuss, then lecture some more.) You can do any one of several things, of course, depending upon the situation. There is no pedantic order about "best" ways to respond, and when. The Holy Spirit will guide those who seek his aid. But unless the teacher indicates otherwise, you may become the immediate inquirer. You have been waiting eagerly for the chance: "Bill, you said that David had very little chance to be a real father to Absalom. What did you mean by this?" You may be deeply interested in this question because you have a young son whom you still have time to influence strongly. Or you may be asking this question "for" a friend in the class whom you love as a brother and who never would do anything to open up this kind of discussion. (Here you are playing the role of door-opener, too.)

In the course of his lecture, your teacher may have taken an "unpopular" position in trying to explain God's Word as God really spoke it. When she finishes speaking—and before someone can pounce upon her with negative reactions—you might reinforce her with: "Louise, I know it took a lot of courage for you to interpret verse 6 the way it really reads. But I am grateful that you did it. If we can't find out here in our own Bible study what God really is saying, where can we expect to find it?"

Maybe your teacher lectured too long and

dwelt on too many dull, spiritually insignificant facts. You have a feeling that reaction during the remaining ten minutes of the class period will be less than enjoyable. You fear that the rest of the time will be spiritually uninviting to the two visitors whom the class is trying to reach. And so—if no one else moves to the rescue—you become class morale builder. Seize upon the most spiritually profitable thing the Spirit reminds you of and speak enthusiastically: "Frank, you said this is a very important study for us, and I agree. You were talking about the tragedy of Absalom and David's relationships with each other. I want to hear some of us suggest what we can do, even at this late date, to deepen the bonds of love with our own parents." With this kind of request, also, you become a doer who seeks to help achieve constructive results from the Bible study.

Sometimes you will become a doer in lecture forum first by being an analyst. The teacher himself may want constructive response to take place as a result of the study. He may mention several things a person can do to overcome difficulties encountered in ministering to aged parents. You know the problems you and other members face, so you offer an idea when the teacher stops speaking with ten minutes left: "Jane, I want to make a proposal. I noticed that you said several things about . . . You said . . . How about each one of us with parents still alive attempting one of these things this week?

Then we will share our experiences briefly next Sunday in whatever way we wish. Let's see if what we have said here really offers us help!"

Others roles discussed in chapters 3–5 become helpful in lecture forum, too, when circumstances tell you so.

## The Team-Teaching Forum

You take part in this form of Bible study very much like you do in lecture forum. Two or more speakers may share the time in lecturing. Then you and other class members react as we have just been discussing. Perhaps two or three other roles come into this classroom situation because of the two-teacher approach.

You may find that a thinker or an analyst will be needed when both speakers have finished and do not seem to have said the same thing. And add to these roles that of reconciler if the two speakers seem to have said different things. If one of the teachers lectures on biblical background material and interpretation, you listen carefully and take notes. The other teacher may lead discussion. In this case, you respond in ways we shall explore next in considering "Informal Discussion."

(Your responses during class use of the colloquy in Bible study will be discussed after small-group discussion. For you engage in small-group discussion as the first phase of the type of colloquy described here.)

## *The Informal Discussion*

Informal discussion taxes all your desire and all your ability to study the Bible with others under the leadership of your teacher. Actually, you can reread and rethink all of chapter 3, and this will be a good start toward preparing to take part in Bible study through informal discussion! Some reasons why this is true are that there is no telling what kind of questions your teacher will use to help you and the class discover and face up to the real meaning of the Bible passage under study. And there is no telling what other members will say! For these reasons, we shall consider only a few ways of responding in Bible study which seem to relate especially to informal discussion. Other ways of participating will be reserved perhaps more appropriately for other teaching approaches you may find yourself participating in.

Your main role in informal discussion is reacting to the Bible-related questions and comments of the teacher and other class members. The teacher is using carefully phrased questions to help the class gain Bible knowledge, understanding, conviction, and/or possible decisions for action. You have prepared in advance for taking part in this study. You will not be talking "off the top of your head." But you will (the teacher hopes) be talking. The enjoyment and divine blessing will come as several of you share what the Holy Spirit (and your feelings) prompt you to say about that part of the Scriptures you are studying.

You listen carefully in informal discussion, for you want to answer others accurately. You think hard about Bible meanings and applications. The mental give and take in trying to discover God's will in his Word is stimulating —the best thing you can put your mind to! You find yourself reconciling views and persons during the discussion. You play the inquirer often. You reinforce the teacher here, a reluctant or unclear speaker there. If members aren't responding to the teacher's efforts to draw forth thoughtful response, you may even play the devil's advocate: "Well, Stan, maybe I shouldn't say this. But I think David as king was better off with Absalom dead, even though Absalom had been soundly defeated militarily." This comment should get a response!

With informal discussion, some class member may go too far and may not be just trying to help the teacher stimulate thought. Lively discussion can open the door to inappropriate remarks. Then you quietly act as protector to the teacher, to another member, or to the class identity as a Bible study group. You may say: "Jim, I don't believe Billy meant that. This is not what we are talking about."

Every study approach you and the class take part in may have its opportunity for some act of witness or ministry in response to the discovered teaching of the Scriptures. But informal discussion leads you and the class especially well from study to genuine response. The *will* is in action. You are ready to *do* something. Minds and emotions have been aroused. And here, above all, you do not want to be talkers of the Word only.

## Formal Discussion

You are part of a spiritual problem-solving group when you use formal discussion for Bible study. The pleasure that you feel in being a careful, obedient student of the Bible and its meanings has its fulfilment here. You use your creative mind as idea man in responding to the teacher's leadership and in helping decide the biblical truth to explore. You often become a reconciler at this point, too. You look the Bible passage over with other members. Then you help select the emphasis of your study.

You use your Bible and other resources as you and the class search the Scriptures for information which is important. Next you use some of the skills of informal discussion in helping the teacher and class decide on possible answers to the biblical question. And you use your analyzing ability to consider the strong and weak points of each possible solution to your study problems. Finally, you add your thinking and feeling to the discussion in helping decide on the best answer and what can be done in view of what all of you have found the Bible to say.

## The Classroom Research Forum

When the scholarly Woodrow Wilson was president, he would work until the early morning hours reviewing and approving official papers. Approval was shown by "Okeh, W.W." in the margin. Someone asked him why he did not use the popular "O.K." "Because it is wrong," Mr. Wilson replied. At the President's suggestion, the inquirer looked up "Okeh" in a dictionary and found it to be a Choctaw word meaning "it is so."

You are a Bible searcher in this classroom procedure. Be thorough. Find out in the Bible if it is so. You may want to use some of the research ideas discussed in chapter 2. Your teacher will propose some questions on which you and other members will do Bible study during the session. These questions reflect spiritual concerns of the class. You may want to use a good concordance along with your Bible. When everyone has completed his research, he adds his report to all the others in shaping up some biblical teaching on the concerns which members had. You then join with the teacher and others in discussing what these passages say and mean.

## The Case-study Forum

The case related on page 84 of *Leading Dynamic Bible Study* may recall similar situations to your mind. You participate in this type of Bible study first by listening carefully to the case as read or told by the teacher or another. Or you may be asked to read a printed case silently. Then you engage in some form of Bible study which will shed divine light on some of the problems included in the case. Later you will discuss with the teacher and others what you feel the Bible says about: (1) the case being studied; and (2) certain life situations which you and the class recognize as being important to you and similar to the problems which the case raised.

## The Small-group Forum

Jesus spoke of two or three gathering together in his name. You take part in this form of classroom Bible study by joining with one or more other persons in the class (not over four or five, preferably) in discussing some particular aspect of the larger Bible study topic. Usually the teacher asks you to focus on a particular point of study. Or your assignment may be to decide what passage needs careful study. The way you take part in discussion in the larger class is usually the way you participate here. Of course, you may speak more quietly—and more often.

When the time comes for your study group to report the results of its Bible research and/or thinking, you may be asked to tell the whole class what your group said. Then you and other class members react to what everyone reports. Finally, you help decide—with the teacher—what the summing up of Bible truth for the session reveals, and what response may be made to this truth.

## The Colloquy

A mother wanted her nearly five-year-old daughter in kindergarten, but the exact age was presenting a problem. To the quite reluctant teacher, the mother explained: "She can easily pass the required test." "Say some words," the teacher skeptically said to the child. The little girl surveyed the teacher with dignity and, turning to her mother, asked: "Purely irrelevant words?" You may become a very informed person as you participate in Bible colloquy.

For Bible study through the form of colloquy described here involves you first in careful advance preparation (see chap. 2). Then as the session begins, your teacher leads you and the class to form small groups. There you and others in your group phrase one or two questions. These questions may arise out of concerns for which you hope the Bible study will help you find answers. Or they may be questions about the meaning and application of specific Bible passages. But you simply help the group carry out its assignment.

You may be selected as spokesman for your small group. If so, when the small-group study is completed you go to the front and help form the "questioning" group in the panel. When the panel discussion starts, you ask resource persons sitting together across from you the first question your small group wants discussed. Later you join in discussing back and forth with other panel members the answers which the resource persons propose to the questions. Still later, you join in the full-scale Bible discussion (the forum period). Here you help teacher and class discover the biblical answers and possibilities for action which all of you are seeking.

You may be asked to be a resource person in the panel discussion. In this case, you prepare carefully in advance along the lines suggested in chapter 2 for doing inductive Bible study and preparing an assignment. For you will be supporting the Bible study as an "expert"! The teacher leads the whole colloquy process.

## The Drama Forum

Finally we come to a role in Bible study with others that is out of the ordinary from the usual in active Bible study. Suppose you are asked to be a role player (in the more specialized sense of the term). The teacher may ask you to play the role of a selfish, ambitious, unscrupulous son. Another class member plays the role of a weak but affectionate father.

You will not be saying, here, that Absalom and David were exactly this way. But later you and the class may consider in what ways they were different from the "son" and "father" in the role playing.

You and your "father" go out of the room for two or three minutes and agree on about four points or areas of family living where you two will voice brief clashes as you interpret your roles. Then you two return and engage in your heated exchange, staying "in character" the best you can.

After your role playing, you are through for a while. The rest of the class members now react to your role playing in various ways as your teacher leads. (See *Leading Dynamic Bible Study,* pp. 88–89, 91.) Later you come into the discussion again as Bible interpretations, applications, and possible decisions for action are made.

## Chapter 7

# *Unusual Ways to Participate*

Your teacher may ask you to make some quite unusual type of advance preparation for the Bible study session. And he will be depending on you for it. Taking part in this kind of Bible study will prove not only refreshing mentally for you, but it can open up God's Word for you and the class in a striking manner.

## *The Assignment-Report Forum*

A teacher of young adults was once heard to say: "I wish my class members would read their quarterlies before Sunday." To which a fellow teacher asked: "Why?" The second teacher was wondering if his friend would discover it if anyone did do advance study.

If you are preparing an assignment, you know your teacher will let you put into the class discussion the results of your study. Taking part in this Bible study approach, prepare your assignment as discussed in chapter 2. That is, use this type of preparation if Bible research and interpretation is your assignment.

However, the teacher may ask you to do any one of several things in order later to support this type of Bible study. You may interview parents about their problems with young adult sons and daughters (or young adults about their problems with middle-aged parents!) You may experiment with possible better ways of dealing with your own young married daughter. In class you will share the results of this unique "preparation" discreetly but clearly in studying 2 Samuel 15:1-12. Or you may complete a section of a Bible study workbook the class is using. Later you will share with the class what *you* discovered in Bible study, and what you decided this Bible truth means for you to do.

## *The Debate Forum*

"I don't like to think of the Bible study as arguing and debate," one class member said when the teacher asked him about helping. And he was right, if "argument" was what would take place.

But when you debate or use the "pro-con" approach in Bible study, you are doing something different from traditional debate. You are thinking hard from all sides on what the Bible means, and challenging your fellow class members to do the same. You do not use superficial, tricky arguments. Picture a class of youth using debate forum to study 2 Samuel 15:1-12. Joe says, in defending Absalom: "Well, if David didn't have better spies than to be fooled by Absalom's plotting, he deserved to be deposed." This type of pleading is not what we are talking about. (Nor would a thoughtful young person say this in Bible study.)

Say you are given the affirmative or "pro" side in defending Absalom's position in 2 Samuel 15. You use concordances and Bible dictionaries to search this chapter carefully, plus earlier chapters. Try to discover all the events and circumstances that helped cause Absalom to feel as he did. You prepare to bring out everything in his favor. Be sure to stay on your side of the question! Don't worry about being one-sided or "unfair." The negative side will see that Absalom is viewed from the opposite standpoint and that David is well supported. The Bible is honest in its accounts about great but human men. And you want to see that thorough, honest discussion takes place about a biblical son and his father. As a result of this careful analysis, you will be better prepared later to see that similarly honest discussion takes place about relationships between today's sons and their fathers.

## The Test Forum

A respected Sunday School leader recently said: "Don't call checklists, workbooks, review sheets, and the like 'tests.' People don't like the idea of tests in Bible study."

Well, don't think of this type of study guide as a test. No one is trying to flunk you out of Sunday School! Or embarrass you. Or force you to learn. Think of the instrument you use in test forum as the first part of a game. True, it is a holy game. And the subject matter is the most important one in the world. But if Bible study is to be spiritually thrilling, this challenge to your mind and heart is needed to bring learning and satisfaction.

Just follow your teacher's leading. Mark the study guide ("test"). Maybe this is at the beginning of the study, and you aren't supposed to know it all. If you are reviewing at the end, you are interested yourself to see what you have discovered in God's Word. If the "questions" are prepared creatively, completing the sheet truly will be a game: matching, multiple-choice, completion, crossword puzzle, short essay, Scripture paraphrase—all interesting ways of learning the Scriptures better!

When the forum period comes, the fun increases. All the questions may not have "right" answers. Some answers will be what the Holy Spirit tells *you* the Bible says. The Word may speak to another person in a way that meets his own spiritual experience and need. So test forum is not dry bones. It brings back to you the suspense and thrills of school days when you used to grade tests in class. That was when you began to experience the growing pains of learning with others.

## The Book Review Forum

A generation ago, a small Baptist college in West Tennessee offered a history club to interested students. The main intellectual fare at the monthly dinner meetings was a book review. Grateful students from this campus club still remember the beaming encouragement which the faculty sponsor gave each student as he struggled through the inspiring life and philosophy of Justice Holmes or the exciting events of *Forty Days on Musa Dagh.*

You will also find preparing a book review on the Bible deeply rewarding if you are given this assignment by the teacher. You may be asked to review Elton Trueblood's *Foundations of Reconstruction* in helping to open up a study of the Ten Commandments. Or it may be A. T. Robertson's brief commentary on the Epistle of James. What you do is ask the teacher, first of all, what special emphases or insights your review is intended to add to the study. You will not want to use valuable time in class while reporting incidentals and other points of less spiritual profit. Also, keep in mind the biblical framework in which you will give the review. Then just read the book for pure enjoyment and inspiration.

Go back, next, and pull from the book in outline form the points which you plan to offer the class in support of the Bible study. Be sure to have planned to stay within the time given to you. And expect to answer questions during the forum period. You can offer further insights from the book as individual members react from the standpoint of their own spiritual concerns.

## The Audiovisual Forum

Audiovisuals today insure that "you are there" to a degree hardly dreamed of by most people ten years ago. And the film director is becoming ever more expert at achieving realism in his work. Realism in spiritual perception is what you seek in Bible study, too. Therefore, if you are asked to be a "reactor" in Bible study using audiovisuals, rejoice and be exceeding glad!

In this as in other group study processes, follow your teacher's leading. He will "set up" or introduce the film or recording or TV program for the class. He will show the connection between the audiovisual and the place in Bible study where you are. You simply do your best to carry out the observation/reflection assignment which you accept from the teacher.

When the film or recording is over, you report your thoughts and feelings as others report theirs. Then all of you go further in Bible study. This way of gaining insight into Bible truth and its application for today can bring you thrilling spiritual illumination found in hardly any other way.

## The Group Conversation

Your teacher may use group conversation to

begin the session. He wants to help the new Sunday School class or several new members get acquainted and on a "communicating" basis for genuine Bible study together. In your class there may be a few persons like President Calvin Coolidge was always reported to be: A man of few words. On the occasion of a smart dinner party in Washington, a socially prominent woman was sitting next to the President. "Oh, Mr. President," she said vivaciously, "you are so silent. I made a bet today that I could get more than two words out of you tonight." "You lose," the President replied.

Your spiritual task in group conversation is to respond promptly, simply, freely, and sincerely. You will be asked by your teacher to reminisce, to go back through the years and talk about experiences of long ago that nearly everyone had. The blessing of this uniting experience for the new group or new members comes as you and others join in the conversation gladly: "Yes, Sam, I do remember the happy days we had in the Junior department back in our little church. We used to challenge the Intermediates to an attendance race for a month. And the whole church enjoyed our friendly rivalry as they saw more and more boys and girls coming for Bible study." . . . "Mary, the thing I used to enjoy most at home was playing games in the spacious front yard under the trees . . . " And so on.

When you have talked with others in the

class about things that all of you can talk about with warmth and genuineness, you then can talk better with them about the less familiar subjects of God's Word and problems of the spiritual life.

## Brainstorming

Don't ever feel that brainstorming in Bible study is a waste of time. Thomas A. Edison, you remember, conducted 20,000 unsuccessful experiments trying to find a substitute for lead in storage batteries. A reporter once asked him: "Aren't you discouraged by all this waste of effort?" "Waste?" he shot back. "Nothing is wasted. I've found 20,000 things that don't work."

Not everything you name when your teacher calls for possible answers to a biblical problem will work. But what if just *one* idea that you (and the Holy Spirit) propose adds a depth to the Bible study? What a thrill you feel! And so your role in brainstorming is simple: Understand the teacher's question or request, and start talking as quickly as your heart and mind will go. You will surprise even yourself!

## Circular Response

Please don't "pass" like the bright high school freshman did when you find your teacher using circular response to stimulate thought and involvement with God's Word. The English teacher had asked the class to write an essay that morning on "The Most Beautiful Thing I Ever Saw." The least aesthetic—and perhaps most lazy, but not most dumb—boy in the class finished his paper with astonishing speed and promptly handed it in. The paper was indeed short and to the point: "The most beautiful thing I ever saw was too beautiful for words."

Your spiritual contribution in circular response during Bible study is to say something constructive when it comes your time in the circle (or on the row) to speak. Your most redemptive statement will be one directly in answer to the teacher's question. To the request to express your feeling about David's actual relationship to Absalom before Absalom's rebellion, you may say: "David was too preoccupied to realize—or maybe care—how far Absalom had pulled away from him." Or: "I don't believe I can express an opinion about this. There's too little biblical information to go on." Or you may react to what someone in the circle before you has said. But for goodness sake don't say: "I don't know" or "Jack has already said what I was going to say" or—"You lose!"

## The Unsigned Written Survey

"I wish I felt free *just once* to say in our class what I really want to say!" Have you ever felt this way?

A Sunday School teacher quite appropriately used an unsigned survey one morning during Bible study to see what the class felt the church needed most, spiritually. One slip of paper came back: "The pastor's resignation." The teacher handled this response as casually and receptively as all the others, but did not take up the point for discussion.

This teacher had asked for honest responses. The class member had given an honest response (as he felt it). The response was received with honesty. Incidentally, that class member, thus "out on a limb" even though voluntarily, faced up to his attitude toward the pastor. Soon he decided he was wrong, and he made a public rededication of himself to his Lord, to his church, and to his pastor's leadership.

Here is your chance to give honest thoughts and emotions as they come to you in Bible study. What a cleansing, liberating feeling can come during such an experience! Be sure your slip of paper has something on it when responses are collected. The Holy Spirit can lead the teacher to make undreamed-of, beneficial use of your reaction if it is a direct response to the question and if it is truly what you think or feel.

## *The Reaction Group*

Here is another Bible study approach where you put forth an extra effort to respond directly as the teacher requests. Three of you may be listening to your teacher's ten-minute lecture. *You* have been asked to make a note of anything you hear or think of that you *don't un-*

*derstand.* Martha is to listen for major points which she values so highly that she wants to *reemphasize.* Sally is to jot down everything she hears the teacher say that she *disagrees with* or even *mildly questions.*

So you see that you want to think straight and hold to your biblical course as you write down your reactions to the lecture, panel, film, or whatever. Later, in the forum period, you can step out of your role and ask or say whatever you wish concerning Bible facts, interpretations, or applications.

## *Picture Study*

Your Bible study can be enriched tremendously when your teacher is using this group-study aid. If the picture is well chosen, you can get much from it of spiritual value. For much went into the picture.

Of course, not all pictures of apparent value will yield much for Bible study. Samuel F. B. Morse wanted to believe himself a painter, before he invented the telegraph. Once he invited a physician friend to come and view his recently completed painting of a man in death agony. "Well," asked Morse in anticipation after the doctor had looked at the picture carefully, "what is your opinion?" "Malaria," said the doctor.

But you may be carefully analyzing 2 Samuel 18:33. You can go further in feeling with David the agony of the hour if you will study carefully a fine painting of David at this moment done by one whose own soul knew a father's love and suffering. You look at the face of David as the biblical background remains in your mind. You say to the class what you see there of grief, remorse, pain, generosity, love. If you had pictured David looking otherwise at this tragic moment, you say so. Others in the class will say what they feel.

If the picture is of another Bible event, you say whether the painter interpreted the scriptures as you understand them. One class member was browsing through an old store and saw a picture of a beautiful young woman—an angel—ministering to Jesus in the wilderness. The next day, the member heard his teacher say: "Of course, you know that all angels in the Bible are men." Picture study can prove stimulating and challenging as you verify the way the artist has represented the Bible situation.

## *Reflection-Response*

It may seem as though much of the responding which we have been discussing is of the spontaneous kind. But you remember what we said in chapter 3 about listening. Patience in classroom discussion is a virtue that brings rich rewards. You can rush the clock and make it strike before the hour. You can tear open the rosebud before it is ready to bloom. But a unique satisfaction comes from hearing a biblical question posed, letting others express themselves, and then voicing your own feelings only after they have matured with the benefit of what others have said.

In reflection-response, you deliberately take time to read a Bible passage and ponder its meaning. Or you are given time by the teacher to consider a statement or a problem before you respond. You even may trace a reference or two in your Bible during the brief reflection period. Your thoughts, for instance, about Absalom's attitudes make you want to verify just how he was forced to flee Jerusalem after killing Amnon.

Thus you see that reflection-response is one of the most satisfying study procedures you can engage in during classroom Bible study. You may spend more time thinking seriously about God's Word and its meaning for you during these two or three minutes than you do elsewhere all the week!

## *Testimonies*

To express your spiritual testimony before others does not make you an odd-ball or a religious fanatic. And do not feel that your testimony is too insignificant to add meaning to the Bible study.

During the decline of the Roman Empire, a barbarian horde from the north attacked and laid siege to one of the great cities of the Romans. A group of citizens of the city, realizing that they could not long hold out against the barbarians, asked for a truce. They met with the barbarian leaders and sought to placate them, hoping to save the city and their wives and children. The Romans took with them to the conference a vast treasure of silver and gold which they offered to the barbarian chief if he would spare the city. The barbarian shook his head. As the sorrowing Romans turned to go back to their doomed homes, one of them, quite by accident, pulled from his pocket a soiled piece of red cloth. Immediately the face of the barbarian chief lit up. He indicated to the Romans that if they would give him the piece of cloth, he would spare their city. Quite delighted, of course, the Romans complied.

When the teacher—or the situation in class —calls for you to voice your testimony, trust the guidance and blessing of the Holy Spirit. The smallest effort on your part could offer redemptive help to the one sitting next to you.

## *Reflection-Prayer*

You will notice that these brief chapters began with a call to prayer as you prepared to take part with others in Bible study. They end with a call to reflection and prayer as the Holy Spirit speaks to you through the Word and through serious Bible study with others.

Your teacher has invited you and other class members to engage in reflection and prayer. And so you assume your favorite reflection-prayer attitude. You may prefer to bow your head and close your eyes. You may want to look out the window or in your Bible or at the floor. Your teacher may invite everyone to use a certain approach.

You pray for enlightenment, for whatever is on your heart. You reflect upon the truth in the Bible study which seems to touch you most. You reflect upon the burden which the teacher has placed before the class. And you pray that Christ's will may be done in your life and through you.

# CHAPTER 8
# *Hindrances (and Cautions)*

"The most skilful teacher is at a loss with a group of irresponsible members," one student of learning groups has said. Whether this statement is altogether true or not, let us not debate. But perhaps we will agree with the statement made earlier in this book: good class members make good teachers.

Members can become a hindrance rather than a help to the teacher and class if potentially good participation goes wrong. And they lessen their own enjoyment of the Bible study experience, too. How can all the good Bible study roles that we have been discussing go wrong? In this chapter we look at some of these hindrances to satisfying Bible study. Then in chapter 9 we will consider some antidotes to these ills.

## *Overdoing It*

It has been said that some vices grow out of great virtues. You can "kill the goose that laid

the golden egg" of the spiritual enjoyments we
have talked about. And these may be only mistakes of the *heart,* not intentional.

A young boy once was enchanted with the
beautiful singing of mockingbirds in his yard.
He decided to put a half-grown bird in a cage
and have a young musician all his own. On the
second day the young bird was in the cage, the
boy saw its mother fly to it with food in her
bill. The next day, the little warbler-to-be was
dead. Later the boy learned that mother mockingbirds have been known to feed poison berries
to their young, upon finding them in a cage.
Something told them it was better for the
young birds to die than live in captivity. And it
is possible to feel so good in the liberating experiences of stimulating Bible study with others
that we overdo our roles and spoil the experience for everyone.

Maybe we just forget ourselves at times. Did
you ever say something in a group that received
extremely warm approval? And then you were
tempted to go on and try to outdo your first
statement—to push your luck? Look back over
chapters 3, 4, and 5. Notice again the roles you
can play in Bible study with others that bring
enjoyment—prayer, listener, morale builder, and
the others. Now consider how easily—and inno-
cently—you can go too far with each one.

Even when you settle down in class and want
to *pray* a moment for the Holy Spirit's guid-

ance, you can be ostentatious if you aren't careful. You can *listen* so long that you can actually become nonresponsive, from the teacher's viewpoint. Your *morale-building* role can become superficial "goody-goodness" if begun too abruptly, done too often, or carried too far.

In your desire to help the teacher *explore* possible interpretations, you can dominate discussion. As an overly enthusiastic *idea man* for possible avenues of Christian action, you can seem to "take over." As you try too hard to *reinforce* other class members or the teacher in their feelings about a passage, you can become too "Sir-Galahadish" (as though the emotional survival of everyone else in the class depends on you).

*Testifying* can become not only ostentatious but too detailed for discretion or for the time remaining for Bible study. As a dedicated *thinker* about what God is really saying in his Word, you can appear to your fellow class members intellectually snobbish. You can even become contentious if you don't watch out.

The *inquirer* can be a nuisance if this is the only Bible study role he plays and he plays it too often. The *door opener* can become tactless in his determination to open up a subject or to rescue the class from endless lecture. The *devil's advocate* can be indiscreet and cause weaker members to stumble if he goes too far in selecting doubtful interpretations to support or in supporting them too long. The *protector* can be unkind in his effort to be kind if he uses unspiritual reasoning and methods in his role.

In your *analyzing,* be careful not to become a bore, substituting the dry bones of dissection for the motivating truth to be found in the Bible verse. And when you are helping the teacher and class with some special study process like *role playing,* you will want to take care lest your performance become superficial or insincere. Role playing is fun, but it is not just play.

Finally, remember that in playing the role of *doer,* zeal for obeying Christ can lead to actions of poor judgment and spiritual "forcing" of fellow class members. Even in this final test of the genuineness of Bible study—obeying the Word —a good thing can be overdone.

## *Misfiring*

We have seen that innocent errors of the heart can prove a hindrance to satisfying Bible study with others. Now consider for a few moments how mistakes of the *mind* can prevent full spiritual enjoyment of Bible study.

"Misfiring" includes all that broad range of circumstances with a gun that causes a bullet not to hit its intended target. First of all, the hammer just may not hit the cap, or the spark may not touch the powder. And through inattention in the Sunday School class, what the teacher or class member has said just may not have registered in your mind. This statement is not a sermon whereby you are chastised, however. You may have been very properly preoccupied, or even in prayer. But we simply are saying that it is a hindrance to classroom Bible study when you don't hear what is being said and thus cannot even begin to reflect upon it or respond to it. A potentially pleasant, satisfying experience for you and the class fades at this moment.

Or maybe you did hear what was said, but for some reason (which we shall discuss shortly) you did not respond accurately. Your teacher has explained how group conversation works and has called for responses. So you say: "I think conversation is an excellent way to get acquainted." Your response is "way out in left field." You were supposed to begin talking about some experience back years ago in your childhood. Or one of your class members has just said: "I would like to hear what Frank says about how David managed his household." You (Frank) reply: "Well, I think a man has a duty to manage his family well. Paul said this, himself." A true statement, but again out in left field. Profitable Bible study bogs down with inaccurate responses like these.

Sometimes in Bible exploration you can be engaged in a case study. You tell yourself you are right on target with the teacher and the kind of response that will help the Bible study. So you speak up promptly and are going fine at first. But then your response strays: "Well,

David was a man of God. No doubt about it. But he didn't manage his household well. For instance—well, I once knew a man right in this town . . . " Off to a good start, but then going wide of the Bible study point which was David. This kind of block to good discussion can occur easily during that excellent Bible study process, informal discussion.

The English writer Jonathan Swift is said to have arrived in his travels at an inn where the lady in charge suddenly was overcome by the honor of having such a distinguished visitor. "Will you have an apple pie for dinner, Sir? Or a currant pie? Or a plum pie? Or a pidgeon pie, Sir?" she eagerly and flippantly urged of him. "Any pie," replied Swift, "but a mag-pie!" (The magpie, a bird that is an endless, inharmonious chatterer.) Whatever you do, don't justly be accused of thoughtless remarks in Bible study with others. Time is too precious. Enjoyment for the teacher and other class members flies fast away on the wings of unrelated, inappropriate comments. Perhaps the book review forum and the audiovisual forum provide special temptations to stray from the Bible study purpose and follow after interesting irrelevancies.

At one time in class discussion, it may be very appropriate to say that "the rascals in Washington" provide a good illustration of the way conditions were in Israel during Amos' time. But when you say several times during the session that this verse and that verse refer to these same scoundrels, you may wonder if you are hung up on just one thing—"the rascals in Washington." To fall into this mental trap causes a serious misfire in discovering the meanings of God's Word for yourself and your class members. Especially is this kind of obsession harmful when the "One-note Johnny" response occurs toward the end of the Bible study session. For this is when the class is seriously exploring what to do in response to the discovered teaching of the Scriptures.

## "Don't Want To"

Here we are referring to moods and attitudes which you can drift into that hinder enjoyable Bible study with others. At this point during the class period you just don't *want* to join with the teacher and others in "serious, inspiring Bible study." Your reasons (or the causes) may be many. (And you are not now about to be flogged for them. In chapter 9 we will consider some antidotes for these Bible study ailments).

You simply may not like the teacher. And you do not yet possess the grace and maturity to overcome this feeling for the sake of fellowship and harmonious Bible study with the class. So you come to Sunday School and say nothing. Neither informal discussion, circular response, or any other thought-provoking procedure can draw you out.

Or maybe you like the teacher fine. But on this occasion, you do not feel spiritually ready for such personal experiences with God and others as the procedure, prayer-reflection- report, calls for. And so you are unable to enjoy participating in Bible study this way right now.

But before we go a bit further in this vein—and perhaps lose you—let's recognize that sometimes you don't want to participate because *you're just plain tired!* You need as much quiet and rest from the week's work as you can get, but you did come to Sunday School. And if everyone else had been up until three o'clock in the morning trying to sober up an alcoholic friend, they wouldn't feel so lively, either! You don't have to have something "wrong" with you to keep you from feeling like taking part in class discussion on a given occasion. When the teacher asks you to be a role player or to lead off in an informal "debate" or pro-con discussion, you just don't feel up to it today.

You may not be able to plead fatigue every time you decline to be a role player or a small-group discussion leader, however. Maybe you are an extremely self-conscious person and so you just aren't ready to venture out yet. Even though this fact explains your situation, the total enjoyment of the Bible study experience still is limited for you and the class by your failure to respond. (We are not saying that ultimate satisfaction for everyone during the session is spoiled by your declining to participate, of course. The group is too mature to refuse you the privilege of reacting as you feel you must.)

Again, you may not trust the teacher, the class, or the situation with your feelings. Perhaps you have seen a teacher hand out pencils and slips of paper for members to write their unsigned reactions on. And one member just sits there with the paper in his hand, doing nothing. He also may not be sure he wants to intrust his innermost thoughts to this kind of situation. He just isn't sure. So he writes nothing and hands in his blank sheet with the other responses. When you are the "he" in such a situation, this lack of trust can prove a stumbling block to a refreshing spiritual experience in Bible study for you.

Have you ever been in a Sunday School class situation when you felt on the defensive? Insecure? This feeling also is one into which you easily can fall. What if the class is discussing David's relationship to Absalom, and several members know you are having trouble with your own twenty-year-old son. You just don't feel qualified to say anything about David when you are having the same trouble yourself. When the teacher uses circular response and it comes your time to comment, you just don't want to. Consequently, the link of class exploration of Bible meanings is broken for the moment.

Another pitfall to satisfying Bible study can appear in situations like small-group study and classroom Bible research. Do you ever feel happy-go-lucky, reckless, rowdy in a group situation where you may feel a little unsure of yourself, or impatient with the procedure being used? You make wisecracks, say "hostile" things that are only thinly veiled, or continually raise problems about the assignment. Clearly this don't-want-to mood can cause you and the others to lose some of the enjoyment of Bible study.

"That's old Joe for you," the class president said to the teacher after Sunday School. "You can always count on him to raise some kind of doctrinal problem." Do you feel that your class members have you tabbed? Have you assumed a "fixed role" in the class so that members always know what to expect? You just don't want to make any other kind of contribution to class discussion. If this situation is true, you are missing some of the pleasures of playing other roles in Bible study.

You certainly get out of patience, sometimes, with the working out of a classroom procedure the teacher is using. Formal discussion in Bible study, for instance, involves five distinct steps. If you don't see the value of each step, or if you are "way ahead" of the rest of the class, you can become impatient. When this occurs, enthusiasm for the Bible study fades, doesn't it?

Assume that you are some kind of study leader. What is the most devastating thing a panel member can do to you if you have tried to prepare a stimulating panel discussion? It is to neglect to do anything about it, isn't it? Maybe your Sunday School teacher is using assignment-report this morning. Your job was to do Bible research and prepare a background report on Absalom's parentage and early life. Class discussion now is in full swing, and the teacher calls for your report. You lamely say: "I'm sorry (you aren't very much), but I don't have it." You don't go on to explain, probably, that you neglected to do the Bible research because you didn't want to. Suffice it to say, happiness-in-Bible-study for you and everyone else is marred at this moment.

Does all this sound too depressing and critical to you? Then let us move quickly to chapter 9 and more constructive thoughts on enjoying Bible study with others. How can you move toward overcoming these hindrances to satisfying Bible study? How can you grow spiritually as you develop the ability to take part in Bible study in many of the ways we have discussed in this book?

# CHAPTER 9
# *Antidotes*

The great painter Millais was seen on one occasion leaving early in the day from an elaborate exhibition of his works. A friend noticed tears in his eyes. Asked by the friend what was the matter, the master replied: "I am so ashamed, in looking at the work of my youth, that I have not fulfilled that promise in my maturity." How many of us could make this admission? If we are to grow in the ability to share with others our thoughts about God's Word, we shall begin in true humility.

## *Avoid Overdoing It*

Check up on yourself even during the Sunday School class discussion. Ask yourself if you are carrying your Bible study role too far. Slow down a little. Pray with your eyes open. God reads the heart and mind, not the eyeballs. Withhold your morale building until you sense that it's really needed. And base your thrust on a strong spiritual concept rather than a

superficial "Don't we enjoy being together!"
Use self-control as Bible study idea man. Say to
yourself with firmness: *"One* good suggestion.
That's all! Then let others give their ideas."

To yourself as reinforcer, say: "Wait a minute. You've said enough for now. The whole
success of every person's experience this morning in Sunday School doesn't depend on you!"
Watch others as you give your testimony. If
you are becoming too detailed, little things that
the members and the teacher do will let you
know. Like the teacher fumbling with his notes,
or a class member shifting position and scratch-
ing his head nervously.

If you have taken too intellectual an approach to a simple Bible truth, the glances of
members to each other may let you know. You
can check yourself if you are becoming contentious: "Have I come back again and again in
direct response to another's statements?" At a
point like this, you may discover that you have
violated the spirit of the Bible study group. Do
not berate yourself. Don't withdraw from the
discussion in a mood of guilt. Be reassured by
your intentions. If "the road to hell is paved
with good intentions," so is the road to heaven.
Just slow down a little. Meditate. Pray.

Of course, if you say something tactless and
unkind while helping open the door to more in-
vigorating Bible study, apologize on the spot!
The other class members may need to see the
refreshing experience of a Christian who can

apologize freely, fully, and with love. This old thing about "you don't have to apologize" blocks spiritual communication and prevents wounded hearts from healing quickly.

Improving along the lines that we are talking about here requires a little planning on your part. Once Dr. Dooley of Africa and Laos was talking about Christian progress with Albert Schweitzer. "Men need a program, Dr. Schweitzer," insisted Dr. Dooley. "No," replied the older man, "all you have to do is give men a feeling of awareness, that's all." But Dr. Dooley was right.

You are aware of your need to improve in Bible study participation. But you will grow faster and enjoy it more with some plan.

Recall Benjamin Franklin's project for personal improvement: He made a list of ways in which he wanted to improve. Then he worked on each of these weaknesses one by one, concentrating on each one for a period of time until he had corrected it. You can do the same thing week by week as you deliberately keep in mind these enjoyable ways of taking part in Bible study—that you are *not* going to overdo!

### Avoid Misfiring

Goofs in the Sunday School class need not distress you. You are certainly in good company. And your slight misfortune often gives the teacher and members a good laugh—a spiritual blessing in itself.

One of the best ways to avoid the kind of misfires in class discussion that we mentioned in chapter 8 is to *listen carefully*. You just can't miss responding with a fair amount of accuracy if you hear clearly what is said and understand it. You can always ask the speaker to repeat what he said. In the last analysis, you can say "I don't know." But you don't want to say "I don't know" to something you do know.

Again, you can avoid irrelevancies by shutting out unrelated thoughts and concentrating on the Bible point being discussed. Did you ever walk into a telephone booth and try your hardest to get the light to come on? Finally, you realized that all you had to do was shut the door tightly. Then the light came on. More clarity and understanding come in Bible study when outside thoughts are shut out. Then you can think about the Bible passage and what others are saying about it.

The thing that will help you here is your knowledge that you do want to grow in the ability to study and discuss God's Word with others. Someone once asked Charles Lamb if he was musical. Lamb answered: "Sentimentally, I am disposed to harmony; but organically, I am incapable of a tune." Responding to others with satisfaction in Bible study is a spiritual art in which you can cultivate skill. You are capable of dialogue in spiritual matters the same as you are in the art of cooking, farming or fishing. It is a matter of staying relaxed and becoming at home in the discussion of God's Word.

What is one of the first things a football coach trains his players to do in the early fall practice? To fall easily. To not get hurt. To get tackled and get up again uninjured. You will want to smile and try again when you misfire in Bible study with others. Your fellow class members will understand. They will be trying to learn how to fall easily themselves.

## *Avoid "Don't Want To"*

"A church is not a museum, an exhibition of saints, a showing of pious purebreds," said General Ensley. "A church is a school, a group of people in various stages of development from beginners in the Christian life, with the dirt of the world still on them, to those clad in the white robes of the saints." Cannot this also be said of your Sunday School class? Only you may say that you are not in the white robes of the saints! But you can accept yourself as you are in your desire to relate to your fellow believers and grow in the grace of Bible study.

Try to develop a deeper love for God's Word. You then will want to discuss it with others. This Word will enrich your whole being. John Ruskin said that the memorizing of the Bible which his mother led him to do as a boy accounted for whatever greatness there was in his writing. When you spend time with the Bible before class study, you will feel more at home with it when discussion begins.

If you don't feel at home with your class members, go to more of the class picnics, class meetings, and other social activities with them. It is true that strangers find it rather difficult to enjoy Bible study together. You will be less self-conscious and defensive around persons on Sunday morning who, you learned at the picnic, really like you now but didn't know you before. You will trust a teacher not to hurt you with unsigned survey slips whom you have appreciated over the dinner table and played softball or shuffleboard with.

At one time, the Nizam of Hyderabad had four servants whose sole duty was to dress him. Each servant dressed a different part of the royal body. One man, for example, was the trouser specialist. He would have been insulted if someone had asked him to put on the royal shirt. And when he got on the Nizam's trousers, he sat in the shade and rested up for the next morning's work. The part of this interesting story that may be the most helpful to us is the crystallized role each servant played. You may find yourself playing only one role in class Bible study. Why not give some thought to cultivating one or two more roles? Your enjoyment of Bible study will increase proportionately.

And now about that neglecting of the assignments that your teacher asked you to prepare. If you "don't want to" play this kind of contributing role in Bible study yet, don't accept the assignment. Maybe by the time you are asked again, you will be ready to respond helpfully. Meanwhile, maintain your integrity as an interested, growing Bible student by not accepting anything you don't intend to do. Thus you will be on solid ground and heading in the right direction.

## *Epilog*

Someone asked Thomas A. Edison how he accounted for his amazing inventive genius. He replied: "It is because I never think in words. I think in pictures. I picture some object I want to invent. This picture takes possession of me. It sinks into my subconscious mind and, even while I am thinking of something else, the creative subconscious mind works on it. Soon I get flashes of insight—creative hunches—that produce the invention."

Let the Holy Spirit help you picture the kind of interested, thinking, expressive person you want to be in honoring the Holy Scriptures that you study with others. In a time of reflection, *imagine yourself participating in ways we have discussed.* Select the ones that appeal especially to you. Combine hope and faith with your thoughts: Hope is wanting this blessing intently, faith is believing in its realization.

Remember how the acorn in the gound finally splits its husk, sprouts, and begins to take root. Much unfinished business lies ahead of it.

But in the providence of God, it will one day become a strong sinewy oak. You can develop into one of God's rich helpers of others in Bible study by learning to enjoy it intensely yourself.

Pray that this little book will help you along that road.

# Index